Cosmic Candle

Kindling The Light of Your Consciousness

By

Francois Joseph Jr

Book Cover by Valentina

1st edition 2023

The Cosmic Candle

# Table of Contents

## ACKNOWLEDGEMENTS

This book is dedicated to my parents Jean and Josephine, of whom I am eternally thankful for their support and to my son Francois.

# Chapter 1

## Seeing The Gradient

Man cannot seem to move his thinking away from seeing things in steps and to move his thinking towards seeing things in degrees. Since childhood, you have been conditioned to see things in steps, with each step providing you with a better view, each step elevating you above something or above someone and it is the nature of the ego to be above something or to be above someone. The ego loves to be on top, it loves to demonstrate its superiority. As such, you need to learn how the ego has made you who you are. From the very beginning, everything starts out with baby steps, then you have to take the next step to a higher level within certain scales which themselves are stepwise functions and soon you have become full of ego and distinct in nature.

This is natural running a business for it allows easier tracking of progress and the tracking of business growth. Running a business is systematic, it follows thoroughly developed processes whose steps ensure viability, ensuring viability must be stepwise to prevent mistakes and errors, you are seeking to be close to the absolute nature of running that business. However, when you learn to see things in degrees, this keeps you sensitive to the nature of reality, to the nature of life and when you are sensitive to the nature of reality, you will always seek wholeness, preventing your life from entering chaos.

Seeing things in degrees, the gradient is always present from degree to degree, the way to each degree is always present. You have to know that it is easy to get things confused when speaking of shifting to seeing things in degrees. Some of you may know what a unit circle is from your mathematical studies in high school. In a unit circle there exists three hundred and sixty degrees, but you must not let the mind think that any one degree is superior to the other as you count up to three sixty or that the higher degrees have a sense of superiority. Each degree is really the same, like the spokes on a bike wheel, there is no difference from one spoke to the other, only they occupy different positions within the unit circle.

The ego is such that it wants you to always compare, it wants you to think that the fifth position is better than the fourth. Life is like that unit circle where everything, though different, which find themselves occupying a different position are equal to each other in degree. The only difference is their function based on their respective positions, which helps to maintain the integrity of the whole. Difference in degrees are not to compare nor are they to assign values of higher than or less than. In a unit circle, level, being zero degrees and in tune with the way. Egocentric-ness is represented by ninety degrees, though equivalent in value, is different in scale pertaining to its function.

In this case, to recognize the egocentric-ness, this is the light recognizing itself, ninety degrees is the light being a problem to itself, a sort of vertical integration, an ascent into hell. When the ego is a problem to itself, your lower multiplicative orders become disintegrated, you function in a disharmonized state of being and life seems to play tricks on you. The last time you went for a walk or a stroll in nature, you probably recognized this fact, the lower multiplicative order of the forest and vegetative life forms are deeply integrated to buffer the intensity of the orthogonal nature of the mid-day sun.

The ego is like the sun, though it is a vector, the sun runs orthogonal to all lower multiplicative orders and how the lower multiplicative order integrates life forms has to be understood to minimize pain and discomfort in your life. The ego is the most intense nature of yourself, and it is your ability to move away from the light that is the solution, this is you dropping the ego, and as such you move fluidly with the nature of the low ground, becoming one with the lower integrated multiplicative order where life is found.

When you learn to see everything in degrees, you learn the nature of that which is conducive to life. You learn that when you turn your light inwards, you remove your barriers, you remove your chains, and you remove your shackles. Differences in existence are in degrees, though with different functions, and not in form, hence the problem with the theory of evolution which is a stepwise function that is commonly accepted, existence never confuses itself, and you should not be the source of your own confusion or troubles.

Moving away from stepwise functions, you move into life, you learn that quality is superior to quantity, when you become quality, you turn your light inwards and allow awareness to build the solid foundation below you. The integrated multiplicative order supports you, you become a lamp, and all qualities are then preserved, for the path exists for others to travel and on the way as flow increases when you encounter others travelling the path, this is indicative that they themselves are lamps allowing all to chart their paths.

A lamp is such that the shade of the lamp reduces the intensity on the eyes a direct result of ego-lessness. When the ego is of essence, your repelling nature is strong, egos are right angles that repel, right angles that clash, they are always orthogonal to you hence the eternal conflicts. You may ask, what are the problems with taking things in steps? Life is in the now, the intemporal, an eternal morphing beyond your ability to control. Taking steps implies you control the life process, it implies you can tell existence what to do, it is you moving in a linear fashion.

To function with linear psychology is to know you are always orthogonal to some lower forces seeking to maintain integrity, though unknown to you. You have to be able to shift at any moment and if you have laid out steps, how can you shift? As such, you can only trap yourself when the subsequent step becomes an impasse. Shifting implies the realization of the change in the intemporal, the presence of the change in gradient. Taking steps is purely ego, narcissistic and every time you take steps, you are moving towards distinction and at the same time losing everything else, losing all your qualities, you are decoupling from the Real.

To be distinct is to lose everything, even yourself. You have to see that nothing distinct can have any meaning for meaning is born to that which is non-differentiable, that which is unique. What is the meaning of water? Water has no distinction thus is the antenna on which life is modulated, it takes on all frequencies. If you look at a desert, you see distinction, this is to be bounded by the light, this distinction is indicative of the disappearance of the lower integrated multiplicative order. Distinction is some authority that disregards your life. The meaninglessness of this distinction being superior and orthogonal, has no limit in the sense of its ability to trap you, for it keeps you range bound, and doing so, it transfers its destructive nature to you.

All which lies orthogonal, understand how to enter the mind of the lower multiplicative order, just see for yourself how all animal life is superior to plant life, for the mind being a vortex is itself distinct and there is always greater distinction amongst the animals in the kingdom. When integrity is lost at the lower level, when disintegration becomes the norm, you have entered a pressure vessel, you now function in time or better yet, psychological time.

To be trapped in the distinct, to be trapped in memory, is to be fixed, a condition impossible to move away from. The moment you accept the nature of that which is distinct, the nature of the vortex, you are now the seed which propagates it, you become the vortex. Becoming a vortex, can you learn? Can you listen? Can you hear the cries of humanity? Do not get trapped by distinctive memory systems, move into silence, and when you move into silence, when you make silence the distinction, life takes on qualities that bring value to the collective whole and life moves away from destructive energies that fixes you and life moves away from energies that block your paths. Silence can have distinction for silence does not begin nor does it end, thus its distinction is of the cosmic order, a unifying force.

Through silence, the energy settles, as the energy settles, consciousness awareness takes the helm and intelligence flourishes. Education is failing most, and the value no longer correlates to the quality it once offered. Everything is moved through concessions where most no longer see the value obtained for their hard-earned money and sacrifice. A concession always depends on some channel, on some pipeline, allowing you to play both sides, thereby becoming dependent on the pseudo, becoming dependent on the false.

So long as you are playing both sides, you are in a pseudo reality, in a pseudo reality you can never learn from such conditions, it is simply ego. Drowning in ego, you cannot learn, and so long as nobody is learning, nobody is listening, and when nobody listens, then only conflict awaits. How do you go from recognizing that you are the light with tremendous intensity, to a lamp? It is through non-comparison that the lamp is born, non-comparison collapses the energy and frees you from your identification with form, from your distinction, for all distinction is an accumulated unsustainable differentiation, a constant walk up a hill. If the energy is dropped through non-comparison and non-distinction, then all space is infinite space, it simply depends on the psychic receptivity and the nature of the localized function of the energy. Through non-comparison, the focus of the eye centers on being when the vision of the one is manifested.

The distinct cannot have nor can it live in privacy, the distinct is suppressed, it is a lower form of energy, and its position is fixed. Distinction is the result of accumulating meaning from that which is symbolic. The distinction is a function of proximity to that which is fixed, and to have privacy, a gradient must always be present where life can flourish. When there is no gradient, when the energy is seen, you are as good as dead. This is why when you are bounded by the light, there can be no quality. Osho tells a great story of being "in between two mountains where a river flows". This river is like awareness, you can enter the river between the two mountains and feel its energy flowing, but if the two mountains get closer and form a chain, the river is split and the geometric landscape is changed and you lose the quality of your awareness. The geometric change is a form of distinction that blocks out awareness, it destroys your essence as you move closer to symbolism. Life works the same way, you, being the light, you, being consciousness in form, as you lose awareness, your distinction is like the mountain chain linking itself. You can feel the substance you lack, you can feel that which is the source of the river, yet your distinction is so calcify that nothing can penetrate and awareness remains on the periphery beyond your reach. Can't you see that the distinctive is the destroyer, it has no intelligence, it is merely symbolic and the symbolic cannot harbor the eternal essence of being.

Do not get trapped in the distinct, it is its own vortex, it replicates itself hence the loop that propagates the distinction. Consciousness aware life is a sweet flow of sensuousness that moves life to wholeness when the lower multiplicative orders are deeply integrated. In this state, you do not need to seek enlightenment, it is already yours, just be still and remain a watcher. Your stillness moves you away from the distinction, away from mind, and closer to truth, where there exists no distinction, where there exists just pure awareness, where you move closer to your true center. You have to see that where there exists no distinction, the real is present, where the real is present comparison is dropped as you remain with the river of life.

Have you noticed that when you compare, immediately emotions are formed. Emotions form without you being aware of them. They go on forming with each interaction you have and they build up your character through time. All energy is cancelled through non-comparison, be it physical or emotional, non-comparison expands the space between object to object, between you and that which is compared, therefore non-comparison expands the space from mind to mind, moving you closer to awareness and away from psychological time. This is going beyond mind, beyond the flux and no scale of which to compare is present which can trouble your mind. Moving beyond the comparison, you move beyond time, and you also move beyond that which weighs on you and impinges on you.

The brain is a measuring tool with infinite variations of scales and the scales created by the brain are different from person to person which depend on their experience. When you compare every form of nuance from the environment, you create too many scales for your brain to evaluate, you are collapsing the space needed by the brain to keep order, you are creating too many false meanings from the different scales, destabilizing the mind. See that when the comparison is dropped, you collapse the energy via non-analysis, that which pulls on you whether negative or positive. Energy collapse does not mean the energy disappears, only that your senses are not misguided, allowing you to be free from developing false meaning. Anything which pulls on you with any amount of intensity is pulling on you to compare, for it has bound you, and that comparison traps you in psychological time, it destroys you. Functioning with psychological time, you become mechanical, you are fixed and can have no privacy.

Only that which is fluid seeks privacy, the low ground. As humans, we seek privacy as our psychology and our thinking process is fluid in nature and anything fluid in nature will hide within great substance and great intelligence. Nothing fixed, nothing which accumulates can have privacy for it has already collapsed and its position is known. When you lose your thinking privacy and the ability to think freely, with that goes your intelligence, with that goes your creativity and all your great potential. When an external center exists, capable of encapsulating and taking your privacy, you are now in chains, in prison, like a lake swallowed up by a cave. When you can understand that great intelligence requires a tremendous amount of fluidity, you will come to know that God cannot be made in form. God is not something you can symbolize in any shape or form. When you symbolize God, when you give it shape and form, you collapse not only yourself but also everyone around you who believe in the symbology. Anything fluid belongs to eternity, including life. Life is eternal, it is a function of the intemporal, while memory is ephemeral thus a function of life energy, and life energy a function of consciousness awareness, the intemporal, that which nothing can touch. Nature moves us away from the dangers of symbology through the birth of uniqueness.

Do not plant seeds in the sense that you are seeking to destroy others, for even the seed is symbolic. A master does not meet you with another form of symbology to heal you or bring you books which are of the past. The master moves away from mind, moves out of his own space and into being, allowing you to move out of your own space and into being where for the first time you can see beyond the accumulated destruction that you have harbored internally. Little by little with each communion into being, you move away from the old, from the negative, from the heaviness. In time, the space of this communion expands allowing you the capability to see all that has impacted you. Only then can you remove the negativity. Before, you were lost in mind, now you are found in no mind through communion with the master. Remember, your thoughts cannot determine phenomenal reality, for anything you can think of is just a symbol and the symbolic is only a function of memory from decoding reality in the phenomenal plane. A symbol is only a distortion of the past in the here and now. If existence could not distort your present reality, there would not be essence as it exists in this three-dimensional plane, there would be no physical life forms. Know that you can never move away from a foundation you thought you had, for that would be trying to walk on water, you can only move away from that which you know, and you are always moving away for you can know nothing. Moving into the space of your being is the bridge to moving away from the foundation of the old, the mundane, the fixed, and into your true foundation of consciousness awareness, your true self, your true nature.

Some of you sometimes hear the phrase that life imitates art. But art is symbolic, therefore life cannot imitate art. If you imitate art, you move with the false energy of the past and potential false understanding, you move with the understanding of energy that is not yours, you move with dualistic understanding, as such you are bound to destroy yourself. Everything morphs in this existence and anything that cannot morph becomes symbolic, in such a state it is as good as dead. Do not seek to follow the symbology, learn to move from your individuality to your uniqueness, allowing you to retain both individuality and intelligence where you are no longer in conflict with life. Take the things that are taboo for example in most cultures and see how they fix not only your behavior but also your psychology. Most cultures make sex symbolic, thus love is extinguished. Others make sin symbolic, thus wisdom becomes fleeting. Symbolic means you will be trapped in the energy of that which they symbolize and be devoid of essence. Anything you symbolize, its underlying essence will escape you and frustration will set in. If you remove the symbology around sex, then the understanding that love is a journey will illuminate your being to develop understanding each step of the way. If you remove the symbology around sin, then you understand that wisdom is something acquired through time and each step of the way, you remain aware of its possibility. Life being a journey, you are always seeking the low ground, privacy, a condition that bridges your true potential to the nature of the divine. Your true potential is an understanding that keeps you in the gradient towards truth. With this awareness, you are now ready to create, you are now ready to manifest the beauty from the hidden depths of existence, for you now understand.

Wilhem Reich tells us that "your awareness of being seen through gives you the sense of great danger." This is a very profound statement. Perhaps you have not thought about what it means to be seen through? Being seen through implies no energy, being seen through implies no language, it implies no flow state and no privacy, not even the ability to seek the low ground. To be seen through brings you into open communication with the true source of existence, a unit flow state that is beyond the norm and beyond the known where there is no language to translate this happening.

To be seen through is a collapse of past, present, and future where there can be no thought and no thinking, only the state of entering knowing. All your normal faculties are rendered useless. Existence itself, the true natural order, the eternal is now of essence. To be seen through implies, that which is beyond the light for nothing within the light can harbor quality. Clearly as human beings, this state of existence has nothing of the known and if you are true, for a period of time, you enter knowing itself, no language, just pure being. That which sees through all, itself has no language thereby allowing all languages to be born in its perceived state of absence. It is the perceived state of absence that births the energy.

So long as the perceived state of absence is present, the energy will flow. If the consciousness in form becomes trapped, the energy collapses and awareness is. This is truly the great awakening.

Chapter 2

The Foundation On The Path

In life, everything is equally falling and as such, everything is equally pulling on each other therefore nothing escapes, and nothing can escape. The inescapability kindles the light during the fall, it sets the rhythm in motion whose vibration awakens the intelligence within each integrated function. In this case, all areas are evaluated, and awareness sets the integrative order. The light cannot set the integrative order without first centering around wholeness at the local level. For the light illuminates the path and at the same time is itself the barrier. The duality of the light is truly significant, and you must see why the significance is so. Duality is to calibrate the body, to ensure it can always perform its functions.

Being the light, you are like a lift gate, a drawbridge, a barrier to yourself and to all, you are one sided. Being the drawbridge, everyone can see you, everyone is aware of you and at the same time you are aware of everyone, though you are blind to yourself, you cannot see that you are your own barrier. A drawbridge stuck in the lifted position is not its true function, that is more of a hindrance. The same way, you, not meditating, not awakening your inner light, equally functions as a drawbridge that has been lifted and is stuck in place. You are not only a problem to yourself, but a problem to all.

Being a barrier makes life difficult, and what is worse is when you are not aware of it. To resolve this, a fracture is needed, though it must not destroy you. A fracture makes you vulnerable and that vulnerability turns the light inwards allowing the lift gate, the bridge, to come down and close, alerting you to the nature and power of your consciousness. A fracture is simply mind impinging on mind, but not just any mind. It takes a mind which has resolved itself, which has centered on wholeness, a mind capable of moving to no-mind to fracture another mind and not destroy it. Once you resolve your barrier, once your bridge has come down, you are now one with the way, you are now one with the higher collective consciousness, one with existence, one with super consciousness on the upper level, and the cosmic level at the highest peaks of consciousness.

Mikhail Naimy calls this dying to live. On the lower level, your "lower-self dies and is born to the Higher-Self." Being born to the Higher-Self is to become one with the higher consciousness awareness of the cosmic consciousness. This oneness is beyond the known and its beauty opens all paths. This beauty tunes you to the intelligence of existence, this is not the beauty of form, of materialism. This beauty is you being a witness to the real, melting into life, dancing as one consciousness. Being the light, you become aware of the path and once the path is known, the gate has to come down or else life cannot enter being, spiritual essence cannot become present in you and life becomes a nuisance.

When the light is lighting the path, it is infinitely divided thus a barrier to itself and to all. On recognizing itself as the barrier, it turns inwards, thereby becoming the foundation on the way. Everything is born onto that which can never deceive itself, that which accepts its infinite differences and resolves them, that which from afar is weird unto itself, that which no words can describe nor explain. To explain it, to describe it, is to impede it, but you have to see that it does not exist in your realm, you cannot reach it. You exist in its realm. How can you describe and explain that which is beyond you? How can you describe silence? How can you describe that which can never deceive itself? How can you find the thread to its beginning which never was? How can you find the thread to its finitude which can never be?

All seeds know they are the light thus naturally grow once planted, they naturally fracture, and that fracture, though you see the plant rising from the ground, but this actually a form lowering oneself, the penetration to the depths of that which is, they know they are the bridge to a higher order beyond themselves. Remember, it takes a mind capable of embodying wholeness to fracture another mind and not destroy it. Mother earth is a beautiful mind capable of nourishing all other minds. This is a natural recognition, and though it may seem counter intuitive, all minds must lower themselves and fracture in her presence. As such, all is risen into consciousness awareness, all become a bridge towards a higher order, it is not a question of obeying which is a suppressant from an external authority, it is the understanding that the preservation of wholeness is part of your responsibility even though her vision lies beyond you.

Now you can see that consciousness in form cannot function with free will, it must understand how it fits into the cosmic order. Because the light is a barrier, it is naturally a cause of some unknown consequence whether good or bad, and as such, life is integrative to ensure viability of all life forms, life centers around wholeness so that it may always spring forward, and the integrative function is the gradient towards wholeness.

Now Zen. Zen is the ability to be, and to let go in order to find the way when control is lost. You have to float like a butterfly, to flower, to attract the bees and become non-directional, then the way leads you as you gain direct access to the beyond, the true spirit of life. No conscious life in our environment accumulates in a destructive manner as much as humans and because humans are the only ones that do so, they become imprisoned by time, they become imprisoned by the search for security, they spend their time in computational loops that weighs heavy on the mind. Mind is not your friend, for everything in form is capable of impinging on you.

Have you observed your mind? If you observe your mind, you will notice that you are never at ease, never at peace, and when you look deep within, you find out what you are computing for, the security, the status symbol, the self-importance, you can never achieve them. You simply go on accumulating things which lose value with time and builds frustration within you.

Accumulation implies a form of control, getting trapped in time, and when you carefully analyze your doing, the realization is that the accumulated cannot itself be controlled, it is simply energy flowing. Anything you are seeking to control is deeply integrated into time frames which you can know nothing of. You, being consciousness, you must know that you are not the past, you are not some function in time, and you are not an object. What you are deep down is love, love is zero'th time, it is intemporal, it is consciousness awareness, it is all your energies moving simultaneously in the here and now. You are of the Ultimate, an awareness penetrating time.

Watching TV, it occurred to me that we are swimming in consumption at the maximum level. Everything in existence consumes something but nothing can be compared to human consumption. All consumption is of the mind, the mind simply fixes you, its nature is to accumulate that which fixes your position and as such that which excludes. The mind keeps you partial in nature.

When mind impinges on mind, division accelerates and whatever function you deem as your basis, whether love or hate, in that you will swim. You have to see that you are not a function, a function is something that follows a fixed path and something that follows a fixed path is an object. You are not an object that follows a fixed path. Nothing of the mind is yours and to resolve this and prevent the mind from being destructive, accumulation must be understood in its true sense.

To understand accumulation, you must understand desire and the outward push to acquire that which is perceived to give you value, in a sense that which will give you a sense of superiority. All outward movements are a result of the perception of something superior. The perceived superiority impinges on you, yet that impingement is dividing you in ways that tares you apart. Nothing superior moves towards inferiority, for the greater light understands its order, it understands its power potential. The urge of the lesser light towards the greater is a result of the higher consciousness awareness potential of the higher light. You can see this in full display in the night sky, yet it is impossible for us to move towards any light for there exists infinite space between source light bodies.

The awareness potential opens all pathways as perceived by consciousness, thereby opening dimensions upon dimensions, keeping life in tune with the cosmic order. The awareness potential of our solar system is mother earth, for each source light must have an awareness potential. The universe is not something discrete, it is in open communication and awareness is. The same type of awareness functions in love. Mikhail Naimy tells us that men find unity in women and women find their freedom in men. In unity, accumulation is impossible and thus the bridge is solidified, and life flows, life flourishes, through the flourishment, life is renewed, and the renewal frees the women and at the same time is ordered and made whole.

When you accumulate, it is you that is controlled for you have placed a value on time and as a result, the accumulated gains a value that you cannot grasped and now you waste your time lamenting over materialistic objects. When you can sit silently, existence is happening, the earth is revolving, life is flowing, but you are not aware of it, you are barely aware of your heart beating, penetrating the here and now. This penetration, this flutter, is the intelligence of the cosmic Real in you, a non-controlling motion, for control is not intelligence, control is a function of materialism, false permanence, chaos, that which splits reality and not actually unites it. Heart is your bridge to intelligence thus is not a control.

We all live on earth, and we all have to work. We all have to have jobs, so this is not saying to discard your responsibilities, to let chaos reign but you have to recognize that when control is lost, simply leaving things as they are, a greater intelligence presents itself. Having been accustomed to your nature and your upbringing, to feel lost is the sense of being disconnected from your nature of materialism, to not function in time, and it seems scary as it contradicts your conditioning; however, you'll gain something far more beautiful, far more intrinsic to your nature. You will gain understanding, to gain an understanding is to be beyond all nature of partiality which can fracture and trap you. This understanding is an ecstasy.

When partiality rule you, there can be no understanding for you must now enter again that which you thought you knew, that which you thought would hold you up for good. Being partial in nature, you are incomplete, and being incomplete, you must always go back to the foundation, entering again that which you thought you knew. Repetition brought about by partiality is a waste of energy, it is a constant re-cognition, it is being stuck in place, going nowhere and becoming distinct. You have to see the difficulty in escaping this condition brought about by lack of completeness of information without external knowledge. That which gives you an understanding to move you away from such conditions and expand your boundaries without you having to do any work to arrive here and now, it becomes a transfer of intelligence that unites you with the beyond.

That transfer of intelligence will uplift you, to be uplifted is to drop the conditioning of the past, to drop the conditioning of the past is to drop all scales, it is to move beyond all partiality, it is you maturing and gaining wisdom as you move beyond mind. You must see that when you drop the conditions of the past, the energy fields which cloud your consciousness fall away. Understanding is you seeing what is true for you, that which you stand on. Are you aware of the boundary conditions internally interwoven, giving rise to your self-identity and character?

Picture a rope for example, the rope and the patterns displayed came secondary to the environmental conditions which preceded it. The person you have grown up to become is not a function of your making as the environmental conditions from your birth until adulthood was created by environmental conditions preceding you, by your parents, teachers, schools, churches, the institutions and the interactions with all those you formed a bond, even though it was you that unconsciously wove yourself into the pattern you are today as you selected inputs from your localized environment.

In life, all that exists are simply patterns. You, yourself as you consciously feel your being, you are nothing but a replay of sweet patterns that you have put together through some period of time. If in adulthood conflicts arise, it is simply a misunderstanding of two patterns interacting in close proximity that disrupt the sweetness in you. Becoming conscious of oneself, you realize the need for conflict is never a necessity. The difficulty is that we are comfortable in who we are and the patterns we have created as everyone you grew up with are comfortable with you and vice versa. Only when you leave the old environment do you realize changes are required or else there exists the condition for major potential conflict.

Making change is the most difficult but is necessary. To start, the nature of existence is such that once the mind concretizes information and that information vibrates you in such a way that it takes shape and takes form, you become blind to the rest of the field. Anything in motion has a blind spot, and to function with blind spots in fields of danger creates stress and tensions on the mind. The tension, the potential to create conflict was built in you from childhood. Based on early conditioning, you naturally exclude all that do not align to your views, and this may not be conducive to living a functional life.

Without past awareness, tension within becomes a hindrance. Knowing when to drop tension is necessary to further your growth and development because opportunities normally come in unrecognizable patterns. In the depths of the silent nature of the consciousness Reality of Existence, one comes to realize that there can be no words to describe this conscious experience common to the whole of humanity, but only a state of being in deep awareness out of which all life unfolds.

The quest has always been to understand the nature of the consciousness awareness deep within, that on which our physical existence hinges. You cannot name it; you cannot name it because how can you assign human understanding to depths that neither you nor the collective can reach? There are no words to describe that which cannot be proven yet deep within, one knows there exists a vibration in this vastness, in this void, in this emptiness that gives birth to our physical reality on which we build. You can call it a seeing, and this seeing will induce a pull on the energy that gives birth to time and its infinite languages.

The art of seeing is the deepest form of understanding and when it is developed, you do not speak of gods or devils because those are concepts in time, and concepts in time cannot capture the whole, the absolute. This life is about wholeness and consciousness awareness. It is consciousness awareness that brings out your godliness, but naturally people are confused because to speak of godliness is something they cannot see in themselves. Humanity prefer the concept of having a God and ignore their own godliness. To invoke God is to invoke its opposite, the Devil. But you must see that these are simply concepts and concepts naturally divide and blind you from the Real which can never be divided.

To see is to become one with existence, to see is to abide in the depths of consciousness, and to see is the resonant vibration of silence that gently awakens the ten thousand springs and merges them into one ocean of consciousness. When the mind sees, the mind is silent, when the mind sees, the mind is at peace and at rest, and when you learn the art of seeing, you move away from the mind and into consciousness. Let silence become your eyes, only then the mind can see. You have to develop the art of seeing, you have to know that in seeing, the depth and interconnectedness of all in life are one. You have to know that in understanding the art of seeing, you will transcend your nature of duality, you will enter depths of understanding that seem unreal yet leave you with immense clarity, immense beauty, immense love for life, and immense love for the intelligence that beats your heart and breathes your lungs.

Your intelligence comes from understanding wholeness and the nature of consciousness. Master Osho tells us, "The house is not the walls but the emptiness within, the very word room means emptiness, space. You do not live in the walls, you live in the space, in the emptiness. All that exist, exist in emptiness, all that lives, lives in emptiness. You are not your body, within your body, just like within your house, space exists. That space is you; your body is just the walls. Think of a person who has no eyes, no ears, no nose, no windows or doors in the body, he will be dead. Eyes and ears and nose and mouth, they are the doors, they are emptiness and through that emptiness, existence enters you, and the outer and the inner meet. Because the outer and the inner space are not two things, they are one, and the division is not a real division."

When the inner spaciousness and the outer spaciousness meet as one, then the light of God can only be turned inwards and with this understanding you can see why the eyes of the One, the eyes of God live joyously in darkness. The sight of the One is tremendous darkness, an accumulation of all the energies, a blinding light to those who live and find themselves living in duality. In duality, the impingement on the mind prevents you from having insight into the nature of the one and with so many scales to evaluate, you lose yourself in computation, you lose yourself in quantizing, you lose yourself in excitement through your desires. As such, you can never gain true sight, you cannot focus the eyes to gain insight, to become one pointed. Where the two foci of the eyes meet as one, objectivity disappears. When objectivity disappears, you are lost and are at the gates of your true being from where you observe the reality through the understanding of the cosmic order, you enter cosmic love. You have to realize that you can never gain true focus and true meaning by remaining with the energy, by remaining with your lower self, or by remaining with your egoic center and with the lower chakras.

The two foci can only meet at the vanishing point where all objectivity disappears into darkness. This darkness is a great seeing beyond the nature of dualism. Beyond the nature of dualism, all settles. Beyond the nature of dualism, all embody the nature of God, a direct communion becomes the way, the heart is now open, all is integrated to the way of the One, yet retaining their uniqueness. Beyond dualism, love is found, and this love cannot be broken nor comprehended. Thus, when the two foci merge as one at the vanishing point, it collapses into the vision of the One. How can you quantize the Love from the vision of the One? One whose language is unknown, and your communion is only a silence.

The vision of the One is the clarity of all, it is a sunrise. Yes, though the sight of the one is tremendous darkness but the vision of the one is the clarity of all. This is you entering true being, this is your awakening. In this state of being, "one can see the hidden dimensions, one can see the hidden laughter, one can see the hidden tears, one can see the hidden sorrows, one can see the hidden joys, one can see the unsaid, and one can see that which is unsaid." Amidst the all-seeing, one simply becomes silent, for to find a matching vocabulary of the all-seeing is to again enter duality.

One must sometimes be able to see that the way itself can often times be a failure mode when the energy is misunderstood, the way becomes a control and all controls have failure modes and as such vision is not yours, vision belongs to the cosmic One, that from which you gain your clarity. Enlightenment can be yours; it is your natural state, but vision cannot be yours hence the utmost importance of understanding. With understanding, the gradient flow moves you towards the vision of the cosmic order, this is the voice of existence, that which kindles the light.

When you tell someone vision is not theirs, they will naturally frown upon you as most people think they are in control. When vision belongs to the cosmic one, the weight of existence is lifted off your shoulder. It is understanding and the ability to understand that is gifted to you as such your vision is one with the way. Understanding allows you to carry meaning without the heavy burdens of form, keeping you and your consciousness free. Some have said that life is meaningless and at the same time invoke its true beauty. It is important to understand that without meaning there can be no understanding, without understanding there can be no truth, and without truth there can be no beauty. The dichotomy that life is meaningless and beautiful at the same time contradicts the reality. The real challenge is to understand how meaning comes to be, to understand your center, and how meaning must come from your centering on wholeness. Most never arrive at true meaning which builds a quality foundation upon which their life can be joyous for they do not understand their center and how their center is one with existence. The difficulty in finding meaning in life lies in the difficulty of understanding that your center is nowhere, as such requires constant calibration once it is found.

The natural order from the canopy is such that you cannot claim vision, yes you can claim understanding for understanding function with your senses and your senses when all else is equal, they will not mislead nor misguide you. You stand on your senses; they are the bridge. God does not mislead nor play partiality and Osho tell us that when "you become the deepest valley of reception you gain the highest peaks of consciousness." Through meditation, you kindle the light of your consciousness which birth meaning. True meaning is individualistic, it must come from you and your uniqueness, it cannot be derived from the light of another. Thus, only through meditation that the possibility of discovering the blissfulness of this life is possible.

In life, everything has sight, sight is simply polarization, the condition on which enables us to build great technologies. But these technologies no matter how powerful are limited, they lack vision, for their scope is to control. Vision is the wisdom of existence to you; vision gives you freedom and freedom breeds and moves you towards intelligence. For life to consist of multidimensional time, everything must have sight. Ken Wheeler tells us that "All atoms are polarized, all atoms in their atomic volume are magneto-di-electricity" and this must be true, for consciousness must always have a path towards clarity. Interdimensional flow states require consciousness to unfold the cosmic intelligence through time.

Your consciousness in form is the opening against infinite nature that unfolds the intelligence. Infinite nature is unknown, yet consciousness unfolds its intelligence in the here and now. The problem of modern time is humanity trying to divide consciousness, trying to divide that which is not a function of coordinates. Thus, the only way to divide society is to accumulate anger and hatred amongst the people. Anger and hatred in the path of the Real does not create problems only in the now, but also in the unknow future.

To see that everything has sight is to understand vulnerability, the split between presence and absence. The polarization that often creates deep emotions in you. The emotions themselves are not the problem, you need to understand your attitude towards the emotions. Your attitude is what creates the conditions that block not only your ability to flow, as well as your ability to learn from a situation. Your emotions have the capability to accumulate and the only thing that really accumulates is energy. This in turn clouds your space sense, clouding your space sense, you are trapped in time, and this becomes a nuisance, this becomes a burden.

You have to see the screen of your consciousness which can never accumulate, which lies below the emotions, whose foundation is the presence that dilutes the cloudiness of your emotions. A simple meditative walk outside, in nature, helps you achieve dilution of emotions much faster. To gain insight, you must see and understand the true nature of sight. Only then can you see the nature of foundations, only then can you see how mind functions and how to prevent mind from becoming a barrier, from trapping you in time.

Because you have sight, you think you can see and because you can see, you think you have vision. It is not until you can see the wisdom of your vision does reality moves you towards truth and understanding. Insight is you bridging the divide, the polarity of sight, your insight is existence flowing you through time consciously and when you learn to move from insight to wisdom, life is demystified. Sri Ramana Maharshi tells us that consciousness is "like the blank screen in a movie theater, that on which life is played." You can see how when you accumulate certain emotions, they become a cut-out in that screen that distorts your vision. Such accumulations cloud your judgement of this physical reality, you miss a significant portion of life.

You have to remember that all is in open communication in existence, your clouded emotions which have created a gap in the screen of your reality do not stop existence from uniting, even at the expense of serious consequences to you. The energy never stops flowing, never stops crashing, and consciousness never stops seeking wholeness and it never stops unfolding. Yes, life is a struggle, yes life is suffering, and one should enjoy overcoming the ebbs and flows of life. However, if life becomes painful and you begin to feel the weight of hopelessness, you have entered the hell realm.

You have to understand that the function of energy is to crash, and the function of consciousness awareness is to unfold the higher intelligence potential within you with each passing solar cycle. Each solar cycle crashes the energy and as such the unfoldment of consciousness birth the intelligence which sets the new order, it nourishes the foundation. The energy cycle crashing is to birth the new higher order from the unfolding of the consciousness awareness, the intelligence from above. What is your relation to music other than it is energy crashing? Energy crashing, or what you consider as beats creates the memory that gives you the sweet emotions you enjoy or dislike. If you enjoy the memory, your life is joyful and blissful and if you do not enjoy the memory, your life is hell and painful. You become a pressure vessel. You will find that sometimes life can be a pressure vessel, but the unfolding of consciousness awareness is like an escape velocity where the thread to the cosmic order is always present to alleviate the pressure, for energy must flow and consciousness must live in clarity.

In life, there must exist something that absolutely nothing can touch, that nothing can disturb, you can call it the ultimate fluidity, the ultimate love, or else nothing can exist, and that something is the present moment. The present moment is the infinite, the present moment is birthed of real love and not sensations or feelings, but of truth. The present does not exist, for it is not a function of energy or time. What duration can you assign to the present moment? See for yourself that irrespective of the scale you use, the present moment remains beyond any scale.

The way existence function is that it understands you as you are, and you being a function of the whole, it can never be a barrier to itself nor allow you to be a barrier to yourself, hence life seems to pass by, and you remain the witness observing the beauty of this existence. The present moment flows through you, deeply integrated into the consciousness realm and pulling everyone and everything instantaneously. The present moment, the eternal now has no past, it has no future yet is always here and now, never looking forward nor backward. Now you can see that applying direction to time, by nature, this application becomes its own barrier, and being a barrier, time functions as a pressure vessel. You are not meant to live in a pressure vessel, to be bounded by time, to be stressed and bogged down, hence why you have to understand responsibility as it pertains to the whole, to transcend negative realities. This is why love is so mysterious, and this is why there is so much confusion and mystery.

The present moment is not a function of energy but of consciousness, that which propagates wholeness. The present moment flows through us from higher orders to higher orders beyond us. The present moment is always now and can never be penetrated by human technology, for it penetrates you and as such unfolds you. There exists beyond us an integrative intelligence that is pulling on us that we are not aware of as it is a function of the cosmic whole, and our brains are not equipped to make such connections, yet through mediation, this can be perceived.

The present moment does not exist in time. You can do a simple thought experiment to arrive at this understanding. See for yourself; how can time exist, if by nature it is its own barrier, if it is its own pressure vessel? Why would existence barricade life? Why would existence allow energy, a destructive function, to be the source of the ultimate intelligence? The present moment is what I consider to be the ultimate fluidity, the ultimate love, and it must always be so for it is a function of consciousness. You have to see the importance of love being the ultimate fluidity that cannot be touched, for any ability to impact it, prevents its propagation and the propagation of life, therefore life remains far beyond yet is here now, deeply integrated via consciousness awareness. All in existence flows back to existence hence its function being love and consciousness, thus can never destroy itself as love is its reflexive nature and as a result seeks truth and beauty.

Are you aware, and have you noticed that all that you do comes back to you, all that you construct whether positive or negative comes back to you, and if you can learn to be one with consciousness, one with existence, you too will become love itself, you become the silence which resonates the ten thousand streams into one ocean of consciousness. Notice that in life, anything one can grasp is a function in time and anything you can grasp in time is computation. The very grasping destroys the value, grasping is destruction itself. The mind knows that it is destructive, and silence is its cure, but who can stand the silence? You sit in a room alone and the mind plays back all your memories, and with a mind bent on remembrance of the past, silence becomes heavy. A kind of force that fractures all and unites all at the same time. Silence does not exist in time, thus is a function of the underlying Real, it is always present.

Silence is intense fluidity beyond our ability to differentiate it, therefore it always finds the way in when you quiet the mind. The void is an intense fluidity beyond our ability to differentiate it, therefore it is always beyond you no matter how far you go beyond mind. Fluidity itself in the true context of its integrativeness is the antenna that when properly tuned, allows you to unite and connect with existence. The intensity of fluidity which becomes clarity, this is the love of nature and the love from nature, the love that does not differentiate, the love that allows all to come into existence. The love which exists beyond the senses.

This is the fluidity, the flow state that exist at the heart of mysticism, the antenna pointed towards truth. If you fluidize form, you enter the lower realm, the sex realm. This is a prison long term hence why all in form has a cycle of birth and a cycle of death. Sex is transient. If you fluidize the mind and move beyond the mind, you will enter blissfulness of no-mind, the true state of joy, your antenna will reach God, you become existential, and life takes on meaning.

The present moment is illusive for this is nature's way of avoiding temporal transitional contamination of the intemporal, or you can say, this is how the "Ultimate Intelligence", whom some call God, beats your heart and breathes your lungs. This is how consciousness not only penetrates time but alters the path of the energy function. This is nature's way of ensuring a higher order always proceeds. Everything cannot function in time, nor can life be bounded by time. If everything functioned in time, if you bound everything with knowledge and false understanding, you would have complete and total control over life, which would barricade life itself, you would become destructive, and you would destroy your own foundation.

Anything barricaded is a pressure vessel, a division of multitude. You have to learn to avoid divisions and avoid conditions which pressurize your life, for pressure vessels bounded by time are devoid of intelligence thus you are always moving from chaos to chaos. Just learn to move away from the mind, away from logic and move closer towards the heart and blissfulness will be present.

You have to be careful never to project any ideas you have into the future. Life, energy, and time are beyond your control, and any projection you apply to the future will always be wrong, it is not that you cannot impose your will, for many have the capabilities to do so, but by never being able to be one with the present moment, all the inflection points escape you, and the inflection points are that which truly has an impact on life. When the inflection moments of the here and now escape you, the myriad of gaps created through your desires multiply, the number of variables increases, and all future projections are thus blinding falsifications.

The present moment, because it can never have any duration in time, moves you away from computation, it is design to move you away from the chaotic mind, to help you rise above the computational nature of the energy, contrary to the mind. The present moment is the presence of consciousness itself, but a mind is just a form of fragmentation that holds people to a falsification, it is the result of a type of criminality you impose on yourself through constantly looking either into the future or into the past. To impose the mind to always be a certain way, to hold a particular objective view as a result of some underlying falsity, whether it is religion or any other form of external misconception, is to destroy yourself and turn the function of your mind into a mechanical function, a sort of robotic-ness, and to keep yourself robotic is to be childish forever.

The task then is for you to identify all things in your life that are concepts that are causing you to destroy your own intelligence and bring them to your consciousness awareness. All the things which hold you down, like gravity and temporal events, when conceptualized and maintained through time, can cause the greatest form of internal conflict. They weigh heavy on the mind. Never fight to keep that which you will one day part with, whether it be, mind, words, religion, etc. Awakening that which you love, and it is ever-present, awakening that which you love, it becomes magnetic, it becomes full of conscious light and conscious energy. Full of conscious light and conscious energy, ever-presence awakens all. Ever-presence does not mean it belongs to you, only that the beauty of your consciousness is felt and seen, this is love, unknowable and traceless.

Notice that you are the consciousness that has awakened the energy. This awakening knows it is only part of that which is complementary to the whole, therefore it is only a sense of knowing in you hence why you want to capture it, you want to find a way to keep it forever. Having awakened, life moves with the here and now, fight with it, grasp it, life moves in time, and you lose it as it crushes you. To fight is to interfere, to fight is to act, and all action is fighting, whether be it with self or others. Awakening is love, and love is of the highest order of consciousness awareness. Awakened, you respond to life, awakened, you take responsibility, and awakened, you move beyond burdens and into clarity. All the Buddhas speak of awakening, for on awakening, love is clear, and clarity abounds.

Existence is ever-present in us, for only humans have the capability to awaken to the reality of the present moment and its magnitude. It is Existence that awakens each and everything whether near or yonder. An awakening is not to have dominion over life, an awakening is the purest manifestation of love, it is the first cry of a newborn baby, it is the very presence of

58

existence, the transcendental. Remember, you do not awaken to the light, to the division, your awakening is the transcendence of the light itself, parting with duality. Parting with duality, anything that once captivated you, you are now liberated and free from your imprisonment. The attempt to engineer life is an attempt at accelerating time, it is to accelerate the accumulated boundaries whose nature and composition in time are difficult to understand. Accelerating the accumulated is inviting unknown implications, this is trying to move earth out of its orbit.

Know that, if it can be seen, heard, or sensed, it's already dead, it is simply vibration vibrating off other underlying fields which are already dead, and by you interacting with that which is dead it will only pull you under, hence the dangers of mind. This is why your thoughts are a nuisance, they live in the past but play in the present, taking up much-needed space. You need to develop your mind from an individual perspective and not a cultural one to prevent the malaise of culture from destroying you. The mind, being an implant from centuries past is a dead mind, and this can be seen in using the past to push you forward yet getting nowhere. You can go nowhere propagating that which is lifeless and does not promote life nor is a function of the here and now.

Wherever light penetrates, enters death, the darkness which is abundant in the universe is not accidental, dim-lit forests are not accidental, the darkness of the depth of the ocean is not accidental, wherever life must thrive that environment must be dimly lit, meaning there needs to be depth for consciousness to thrive. There has to be silence, consciousness is illusive for it is the source of all life and is hidden in the depths of depth. You have to work on developing your knowledge of self to understand duality, and to part with it when it is a hindrance. Without knowledge of self, how do you calibrate against the infinite number of things in this physical existence seeking to keep you off balance? Some of which are very destructive.

You have to understand that nothing goes anywhere, hence why you are the light. Recognizing you are the light is a tremendous responsibility, you are the light because you cannot chase nor capture that which is, for that which is, lives in you. When that which is, lives in you, awareness becomes the ultimate value. When you can match the light within to the beauty of your consciousness, life sparkles and illuminates not only your path but others as well. However, when the energy cannot flow, when duality becomes a barrier nor can it remain with the original speed of the Real, the internal intelligence of the energy rises, seeking guidance and wisdom from the consciousness within, giving birth to infinite differences that promote evaluation and understanding.

Realizing you are unable to capture that which is, you awaken, on awakening, existence is present, this presence is the unifier even in the midst of infinite division, even in the midst of chaos there will be no conflict. It is impossible to transcend duality and not create, to not gain awareness, and to not understand. Once transcended, duality becomes a steppingstone to greater clarity. Consciousness uses transcendent knowledge to birth not only meaning but also higher orders. Higher order is not a function of hierarchy but of consciousness awareness, that which is inherent to all human beings.

Anyone can be the source of meaning; it is not reserved for a special few. All chaos is a function of energy, whether understood or misunderstood, particularly our life energy which comes under scrutiny from all authorities including parents and others who would like to control it. The difficulty we suffer in daily living is a function of how we live in time, a function of how we move through time, and a function of what we do with time. All that you do is to support desires that cannot be sustained, to strive to attain ambitious goals which you lack the skills to achieve.

The way to achieve ambitious ideals is not to turn them into goals but to see whether you do not already possess them within. When you look within, the goals often disappear, and what you learn is that goals are in the future, anything in the future rests in a position currently unknown to you. How do you know that when you reach your goal, when you manage to achieve your dreams, and when you manage to pick up that goal, you're not creating imbalances of imbalances? Goals being in the future, sit on some foundation that integrates a time frame of which you can know nothing of, they hold something intact. When you lift that goal, you never know what you are doing or undoing, what you have done is allowing the ego to push you towards greater misunderstanding and not necessarily fostering an understanding of the human plight, hence the term, in time, through time, by time. By the time you achieve anything, it will always be here and now for the present moment can never escape itself.

In time, through time, by time being a time triangle, is what the creation of hell and living in hell looks like, this is what it is to be an animal, and I am sure even animals do not live like this, living with complete unawareness to reality. This sort of robotic living, this robotic lifestyle that we have adapted to in modern days makes life unable to flow without some form of conflict, without interacting with some form of control or gatekeeper. It is easy to see that all is done in time, all you do in time often lacks awareness. It is easy to see that all is moved through time and naturally you will see that all our movements through time are devoid of awareness. It is easy to see that when you lack awareness, you become mechanical, therefore all your movements and function are done mechanically. Moving with such lack of awareness you are unknowingly transferring your responsibilities to third parties who only see you as a data point.

You have to learn to move in time, through time, but the third component which is naturally done without any awareness, you must do so with consciousness awareness. You have to be consciously aware of how you move through time to live life blissfully. The consciousness awareness alleviates the impingement of the time functions. The greater the awareness you move cautiously in time, you move cautiously through time, and by being the conscious entity, all time functions maintain their distance, leaving you with peace and joy. What is the feeling of digging a hole with a shovel? Imagine doing that every day for life.

Now imagine that feeling as a psychological state invisible to you, which you embody. This is what's meant by, in time, through time, by time, you are ever working against yourself without the awareness of destroying yourself. What's the feeling when you're swimming in a pool, a lake, or an ocean? Now imagine that being a psychological state invisible to you that you can embody. That's what's meant by in time, through time, by consciousness awareness. Being consciously aware you live in time yet as you move through time you are ever floating, simply joyous irrespective of external happenings and boundary conditions. Now, which would you rather embody? The latter is religiousness, the former is hell. When you can understand the difference between a time triangle and a triangle with conscious awareness, you see why religiousness is individualistic, you see why it cannot be a function of organized religion. Humanity can never rise to its potential with a time triangle embodying the qualities described above where the individual is working against his or herself.

Chapter 3

From The Present To The Vanishing Point

Modern society is inundated with vibrations from all angles, whether they be from cell towers, radio stations, tv stations, etc. all of which are working against the individual. You have to understand that sound and vibrations move you through time, they push you further in time, a double edge sword bounding either pleasure or pain. Hence their ability to create pleasure as you dance with the energy or to create fear when lack of awareness binds you by time and oscillates you beyond stable ground.

Move closer towards consciousness, the blissful side of life. Ignore the vibrations that seek to condition and lock you in a time triangle where you become a pressure vessel to yourself. Remember, vibrations trap you in the false light hence why we live far away from the sun, yet the distance is enough to allow us to dance and appreciate its life energy. This is the same life energy that flows through each of us. in us, it is a milder form of vibration, a dance you can say. Therefore, as long as you are in tune with the way, as long as you are dancing with the energy, life is beautiful, life flourishes. If this is to ever reverse, where the energy dances you, where you move closer to foundations, you will live in hell.

If time is non-linear, the ability to predict is diminished significantly, and if time is non-linear and you remove the aspect of torture, the ability to predict goes to zero for we are not an object, we are consciousness. In non-linear time the number of variables cannot truly be quantified for they are too many thus the vanishing point remains at a point beyond infinity thus life continues to propagate itself. In youth and your vital years, this creates the sense that you always have time as referenced from within. Even in old age, though the vanishing point remains far into the future, yet knowledge and experience tell you otherwise. That knowing itself creates an oscillation that brings about the fear of death. In linear time, you can approximate the number of variables needed to control any object, giving you the ability to project, and providing you with immense control and power. Physicists have mastered the science of prediction in linear time and if life is to continue, there has to be a shift away from linear time which functions as a barrier, which functions as a boundary, a choking point of life where the vanishing points are cut-off and blurred.

The vanishing point is the integrative function of the whole and requires awareness to maintain its distance in the future as humanity propagates through time, a sort of sloping through time. This slope is the condition that gives you the sense of the passage of time and also what determines the length of time for each, and every species tied to conscious life in the here and now, hence the unknowability of how the future unfolds. As a result of the vanishing point being far into the future, we are presented with infinite differences.

A vanishing point is intense and has an intensity that can destroy you, for it contains infinite variations of rates of time, what you can consider as different scales of the energy flowing through time. Interaction with a vanishing point devoid of a slope kills the future, it becomes a time triangle devoid of consciousness, oscillating between life and death. Therefore, the vanishing point becomes a ledge into hell, hence your intelligence is destroyed. Near a ledge, there can be no suitable flow state that can be an underlying function that bridges the gap in your passage of time, resulting in fear. Near a ledge, it is your natural flow state that is destroyed, you are now either framed, bound or accelerating towards the speed of collapse.

The sensations have a dark side to them when you do not understand their true function in relation to your environment as they can move you through and further in time, thereby destroying consciousness completely when you're unable to turn off that which triggers the sensation, usually from external sources. All sensations are a form of excitement and computation, hence the time triangle and its infinite divisions. The lesser the consciousness awareness in a time triangle, the lesser the quality in the flow of the energy, irrespective of organization or order. It becomes animalistic.

Look at the average lifespan of both land animals and ocean life and compare that to human life which has the ability for self-awareness. Land animals which lack self-awareness seem to live a lower quality of life with a lower lifespan than ocean animals. A time triangle bounded by four corners is the pyramid, the fire within, absolute chaos without consciousness awareness. Hence in the wild, animal life span is shorter for all their function is a form of computation as they lack the type of consciousness intelligence able to bring about true self-awareness. With consciousness awareness, it is pure blissfulness, pure joy, for the fire within is your antigravity, it is that which seeks to link you to the consciousness realm of the cosmic whole which lies far and beyond yet resides deep within. It is that which links you to God, to the Ultimate intelligence.

When conscious beings within the time triangle unite, humanity rejoices, life is renewed, healing takes root, and fears are dissolved. When fears are dissolved, life flourishes. When the consciousness dies, the body is not far behind. Modern society tends to fracture the individual in ways unknown to him or her. To fracture, to categorize, and to shift, that kills something in all as the shift occurs, leading all to judge, compare, and criticize. It's all baked in as a result of division. Where there exists division without deep integration, partiality collapses you.

Categorizing and shifting are the reason the soil is dying, the reason the soil is eroding, the reason racism flourishes, and the reason for all acts of violence. Therefore, all are impacted through time for this leads to the congregating of likeness which robs the nutrients from all roots. To categorize you, to shift you, and to park you, you are robbed of your qualities, of your interconnectedness to the life force. How can you judge that which has been categorized? That which has been victimized as a result of time? Those who are not only disconnected from their physical ground of being but also their spiritual ground of being. One has to awaken and look within, to understand the spirit's life and to mirror those qualities. You cannot allow yourself to become a monoculture that makes you dependent and that forces you to live in fear. When you become one way, you lose everything else.

Consciousness is that which belongs to no category, it is that which cannot be categorized. In the physical realm, we are experts in categorization yet understand none of the consequences; you have to move away from these false understandings and move towards the wisdom of your spirit's life. When you understand the wisdom of your spirit's life, religiousness is born, order is of the essence, all flourishes below, and life springs forth. In the Yoga Sutras of Patanjali, he tells us "If you can control the rising of the mind into ripples, you will experience Yoga." This is a very profound statement, you experience Yoga when you understand your spirit's life as you, the light of consciousness, go from observing the silence of the mind to seeing the ripples in time and through time. This is like a surfer riding the waves, this is you bringing the quality of wholeness to time and energy, both of which are functions of division, yet your understanding keeps you floating above.

To survive something, not in tune with the way, the conditions around the position in which you find yourself have to be understood, you have to uncover the language to find the gaps that keep you in touch with your Spirit's life. We are all squeezed as a result of a greater happening, you have to uncover the nature of the underlying Real, and you have to remove the conditions that bring about hopelessness. Hopelessness is when you consider your last hope to be a sort of solution, but the response provides no relief, yet you continue to go.

This is hopelessness, this is a real pain, and you become a junkie. This happens when you cross time barriers, when you calibrate to the wrong side of form, whether to drugs, alcohol, or whatever is holding you down. Calibrating to the wrong side of form, or allowing duality to calibrate you, your function has been modified, the vanishing point has become a ledge, vulnerability is felt, and during these significant moments, you are simply oscillating and looking to find your footing, to move away from calamity. To see form is to see thoughts and form always implies a fixed position. Occupying a fixed position, you cannot rise above and now it becomes difficult to understand consciousness. Your thinking destroys you, as symbols are trying to rule your ability to break away from the constraints bounding you from developing intelligence.

The moment someone gives you something to think about, they trap your psychology, they have fixed your position, as your mind begins to work on imagining, recycling emptiness, and leaving you with nothing of truth. "Nothing is what you think", and when nothing is what you think, do not give others a blank canvas to restructure your psychology. These concepts are to move you away from thoughts, away from words, and away from the inductive nature of the mind that loops incessantly. It is easy to see that when you move away from a cluttered mind and into spaciousness, clarity abounds.

Clarity is a revelation, clarity is truth, not my truth, not your truth but truth. Truth is individualistic, based on transcending personal experiences. If you find yourself coming apart and falling as a result of hearing "a truth", know that it is not your truth. Your truth is your center and when a truth pulls you apart, you are not centered properly. Take two people coming together, this is Existence's way of alerting you to something far deeper and far greater than you can conceive or imagine. Before you met him or her, you thought you were whole and upon colliding and meeting her, you have fallen in love, when the love fades and she leaves, you are confounded. Now that she has left you, you have fallen far lower than when you were in love.

For the first time, vulnerability has brought you to knock on the door, vulnerability has made you aware that there exists this space within that when made whole, life becomes joyous, life is propagated, and blissfulness permeates all aspects.

For the first time you know that alone, you are partial in nature. Were it not for this fracture, you could never awaken to your partiality, the constraint that pushes you to seek your spirit's life, the presence of the Ultimate.

Now, some people are aware of this vulnerability before any fracture occurs, before other minds impinge on their mind. That awareness abides in them throughout their lives which is exuded in their behavior and character, an awareness that unites them with the cosmic order. Sri Ramana Maharshi, Osho, Buddha are some examples of individuals with an early awareness of the connection to the cosmic whole. This awareness moves you towards the knowledge of Self. Without the knowledge of self, there can be no education, the mind is the bridge towards consciousness awareness, and that which is the bridge towards a deep integrative function of the cosmic whole will not deceive you when properly understood, for the bridge cannot be constructed but of that which leads you towards wholeness. If the mind is influenced by external sources, the bridge starts to oscillate in the worst conceivable way.

Oscillation is a function of duality that sets things in motion. If the mind deceives, then something is wrong in the physical reality from which the brain is decoding information. As a result, you remain infinitely divided, that division becomes a feedback loop, instability begins to take root, you are being pulled deeper into time and away from awareness, and you start to feel closed in, diminishing your ability to remain united and whole. Life on earth is already divided and one should not divide further that which is divided, Alan Watts calls this smoothing rough water with a flat iron, you simply disturb it even more. Dividing the infinitely divided, you cannot stand, and you whisked around to and from. Existence depends and hinges on the integrative nature of consciousness awareness and not divisions. All of life depends on integration, and you as you are now, live on the bridge between time and consciousness. On awakening, you are centered on the bridge, awakening gives you understanding, and awakening provides you with insight into not only your fragility but all that lives in time.

Awareness is common to us all, the only difference that determines the level of awareness within is how you construct your bridge. The construction of your bridge is a function of your love, a function of your inclusiveness. If you build a ten feet bridge, in the realm of consciousness awareness this is really a choke point, and it might even be a nuisance for yourself. If you build a bridge that spans across space with great heights, your centering provides great depth and understanding. You have to ask yourself; can you afford enemies when you live on a bridge? Any rattle in time becomes tremendously stressful.

The breath calibrates you to both time and consciousness, a form of centering that allows both dimensions to expand in the here and now, each interpenetrating the other, renewing the quality. Existence is not about time as we have conceptualized it, the same way it is not about the mind, for the mind comes to be in time, Existence is about you, consciousness. From the human perspective, if existence was about time, humans would not need to be born, animals would be sufficient for the job. It's about that which is propagated through time, consciousness, that which is significant, and consciousness requires a specific quality of mind which can only be found in humans.

Vibrations that resonate in the body are like earthquakes to the mind, destroying the consciousness. Now you can imagine that the duration of the vibrations will determine the damage or impact on the quality of the mind. There's no way that the self can trigger an earthquake that rattles your mind, the foundation on which you live, that it moves to destabilize you. This is impossible, an earthquake that impacts an area, you can assess the damage, but how can you assess the volumetric impact on the psychology of the individual when external forces impact the body and impinge on the mind?

However, if you can operate and function closer to the consciousness realm, you can incarnate to repair that which is being destroyed or has been destroyed. The mind has to see, and all that can be seen lives in the past. Once beyond mind, you can build a quality that always keeps you grounded even through the worse conditions. On a bridge, even if you're blind as a result of computation, you can still keep going but you are at the mercy of external forces. But on approaching reality, you have to awaken for you are now beyond mind and are now operating in no mind, and only once beyond your mind can you see the mind itself. You are the integrative force behind this happening, you have to lower yourself.

Lowering yourself, flow states are sensed, and they become visible. Once visible, you have uncovered the essence of the internal collective flow, you are now the driver. Anything of surface value requires many varieties to be of satisfaction but this is a false sense of satisfaction for anything surface value keeps you walking on eggshells, the true comfort is missing. It's one foot in and one foot out and the sheer force alone destroys you. Before there can be any shift away from the trappings of time, there first has to be a shift in consciousness awareness. It can never work the opposite. In actuality, time does not change, time goes nowhere allowing consciousness to not only function as an escape velocity but also as a true guide, the real guiding light which does not point to any direction. Your notion of time is a result of energy rotating around the sun, the light. When time goes nowhere, you are therefore the light in the here and now. When you get pulled into time, two things can happen, you can remain unaware thereby amplifying the nature of the existing energy as it continues to accelerate or you can chose wholeness or through consciousness awareness, through non-duality, through awakening, you allow the energy to unfold its infinite variety. You have to be able to see that time goes nowhere, you have to be able to see the full manifestation of energy and that only you can discover and understand, it comes from you. Only then can you avoid the brutal nature of energy, and only then can you avoid duality, and minimize volatility.

Remember, consciousness is observing flow states and their many ranges from laminar to turbulent, when you remove the concept of time as we currently know it, duality is transcended and the entropy remains constant, when the entropy is constant, equilibrium is established. There can be no sensation without focused interaction. Focused interaction is any object with mass capable of applying weight, either stationary or a form of motion leading to the feeling of sensation. Only the felt presence of a focus interaction can generate enough mass to give rise to sensation.

The mind, being a bridge, cannot generate surface level friction anywhere on the body, it can command but cannot itself be the source of unwanted vibration that leads to sensation. A bridge is very fragile, a bridge though strong, has limits, and the limits of the mind are such that it cannot deceive itself. Zen meditation is the greatest tool to get in touch with reality and to know oneself. Zen is not serious, that which is serious is focused, and that which focus impinges, and that which impinges creates hell. Zen not being serious allows for the beauty of that which is to be seen and the right sensations to be felt in all things. The senses detect all that focuses, hence too much-felt sensation creates hell for the individual. Any other sensation in or on the body is of external sources. When sensuality transcends all sensation, a sense of ease is present, this form of sensuality cannot be felt, it is Presence itself. All which lies beyond is integrative; energy is integrative hence it always crashes. Through each crash evolves the foundation for the formation of new patterns that solidify the integration of the lower multiplicative order.

Consciousness is integrative, it always unfolds. Through each unfoldment, awareness expands the vastness of your being. Through lack of awareness, all we do as humans is fight the integrative nature of energy and consciousness which contain all the secrets. When consciousness penetrates time, it is simply a dance, no fear, and time takes on meaning as the energy seeks to match the wholesome nature of consciousness, it collapses the old energy and takes on the quality of the unfolding consciousness. It is seeking to be in tune, akin to singing your favorite song, knowing not only the lyrics but also the cadence on which your heart dances, on which it palpitates.

To penetrate time, you have to dance, you have to flow, and you cannot forget to do so, you do not want to get stuck or to remain trapped in time. Nothingness and darkness are so vast that light is born, the depth of nothingness is such that it is only light that can ever cover such gaps and such distances. That light is you, the light of your consciousness. The greater the gap in this physical existence, in this phenomenal plane, the faster the energy have to travel, and the faster the energy travels, the greater death seems to multiply. We are living with too much misunderstanding from old invalid knowledge. This creates a runaway reaction. The mind and the collective psychology contain many gaps, these gaps are results of fields that pull on you unknowingly, and through meditation you can bring about the necessary balance.

Nothing goes anywhere; therefore, you are the light. You are the light because you cannot chase nor capture that which is, for that which is, lives in you. When that which is lives in you, awareness becomes the ultimate value. When the energy cannot flow, nor remain with the original speed of the Real, the internal intelligence of the energy rises, giving birth to infinite differences that promote evaluation and understanding. Realizing you are unable to capture that which is, you awaken, on awakening, existence is present. Presence is the unifier even amid infinite division, even amid infinite chaos there can be no conflict. Presence being your spiritual ground of being elevates you to levels that sustain wholeness, and bridge gaps in the field. This is the eye of the hurricane. The gaps of yesteryear are many and are unknown, but the consequences will be felt in the now at the same time trying to understand as best as possible that which remains unknown in the now.

Chapter 4

Seeing Through The Pitfalls Of Excitement

All excitement is computation, computation is a
function of the mind, and if you learn to understand who
you really are, you will find out that you, being a
conscious entity, do not compute. You are simply pure
awareness. When you are computing, you cannot
transcend as computation is a function of energy, hence
why consciousness remains above all aspects and all
forms or else life is destroyed. Computation is a pull,
tension, and perpetuation of duality that brings about
discomfort. Transcendence is a unification towards
higher quality, where no tension exists, simply the vision
of both eyes united, one-pointed towards the vastness of
Existence. This one-pointedness, in contrast to physical

life on earth which simply loops energy without conscious awareness, is simply clarity.

The looping of the energy without the transcendent nature is just as if you are spinning the physical reality in a centrifuge, tearing it apart, watching each layer, separating and forming over time. Once each layer is formed, a center for each is developed with an affinity for each of the visual qualities of each said center, further separating, further distinguishing, further dividing, and moving farther and farther away from reality. Each one of us is doing just that, made worse in collectivity through time. Even the planet which rotates at great speed is balanced. When you're perfectly centered, there should not be unwanted forces acting on the body. Existence is so perfect that none of its forces are felt other than hunger which pulls on you to interact with the environment.

To create greater affinity towards a specific center and to expand that center at the same time, others must be destroyed, and life becomes imbalanced. Hell descends. Unfolding reality from nothingness with no reference requires true intelligence, requires the ability to record, and requires you to drop all concepts. Unfolding intelligence with the local center of consciousness awakens existence, awakens all intelligent life forms and possibilities.

An awakened intelligence, pointed towards a center, with guidance or a guiding light is simply knowledge, not an unfolding of the Real, which is of the beyond, thus it contains many gaps. All affinities towards a center induce a negative response from the periphery and the collective, it's the nature of the physical reality as it revolves. That negative response destroys the individual intelligence of all those in the periphery and cripples their growth. Once you create an affinity, anything other becomes a problem, anything other becomes a nuisance and must be dealt with.

Absolute reality is of a different function. An affinity is a likeness based on a relationship or causal connection, life is not causal, nothing integrated is causal. How can you speak of divinity yet push for affinate connections? That which destroys wholeness? Computation is a function of lack or missing information and so long as the information is hidden, you remain in eternal computation moving faster and faster towards the abyss thus the mind cannot see yet remains excited. The mind remains excited for it is projecting onto the future its wants and wishes without referencing if the required skills exist. The mind has no ability to see into the future yet is immensely powerful giving its ability to function at the speed of light. If you go deep within, something else far more valuable comes to the surface, something that bypasses duality.

Once you move beyond duality, you do not compute, pure consciousness awareness becomes the guide, and you move beyond the inductive nature of the mind. Moving beyond the inductive nature of the mind, you approach wholeness, that which is whole does not compute yet is complete, it becomes a mirror for the computing energy that brings about order. When the mirror reflects to you the energy, it pushes on it, giving it a sense of completeness, and wholeness, it pauses computation, allowing the qualities present in the energy to unfold. I know in our modern time we are busy with

TV, Instagram, Facebook, Twitter and all the other distractions, but you should go and look at the stars occasionally, they point to something quite significant.

As inductive bodies, they are not in conflict yet are in open communication, allowing all life to thrive in each of the life forces that orbit their spheres. Devoid of consciousness, the mode of computation in inductive bodies accelerates the feedback nature of the energy, shifting the equilibrium point and creating imbalances as it pulls apart the energy. Computation, being a function of missing information, every time you build, every time you compute, entropy increases as that computation is done on the foundation of missing information. Hence when the ultimate intelligence is present, when love appears, all is dropped. Where can anything stand other than in the light of the consciousness of reality? There is no room for discomfort when Existence is present.

Once you home in on your personal frequency, you lose touch with reality, this is a necessity so you can become aware of the energy. The problem lies when the false mirror reflects that frequency back to you. This is trapping you in youth psychology. Culture can sometimes be a false mirror, as it amplifies and echoes the false and soon you have forgotten who you are. When you were a child, you were open to all other dimensions thus you learned quickly, once you started homing in on your own frequency in your teenage years, you got stuck.

Remember, your frequency is based on the cultural output hence many of us have much in common. This lower cultural understanding you cannot stand on, you can only stand on a frequency that's based on your own individuality, your own intelligence, this is the first step. You must turn inwards to tune the selfishness of individuality towards the uniqueness upon which you can pivot that serves the common good. This again allows you to become open-ended to the opportunities of life and all its possibilities, to unfold your consciousness.

The quest to understand individuality, and to be unique is the quest for true significance. The great master Osho reminds us that our scriptures can have no significance without the individual first having significance. Most religions outsource our significance and in doing so we lose touch with the truth. Losing touch with truth, you are divided, and you walk around with deep pain, yet it is only you that can solve your problems. As Ramana Maharshi puts it, this is you taking care of yourself and allowing the world to take care of itself.

Has it occurred to you that you are an individual within a field of consciousness awareness? To be an individual in a field of consciousness means that you are an endpoint, pushed out by the nature of conscious intelligence. To be an individual implies you are part of something far greater than you can perceive. Being an endpoint, awakening brings you into alignment with the greater cosmic consciousness as it observes the energy through your unfolding of your local consciousness, not only at the local level, as well as impact on the collective. The natural response from the individual perspective is to move away from the perceived negativity that has a grip on your psychology that prevents knowledge of knowing the intelligence throbbing in you.

Duality is to protect the body, duality is to help calibrate you as two human intelligent beings, male and female move toward functioning as one. Duality serves as a calibration that gives the body form, the pattern recognizable by all, this is organic calibration. To keep your body organically calibrated, you must have great strength. I have been working on this aspect of internal intelligence and thus far have failed and I'm hoping to one day master it. Now in physical reality, once you are calibrated to a system with functions external to yourself, you lose your intelligence, for that is a control controlling you. Once an external system calibrates you, you not only lose intelligence as a result of being caged in but also consciousness.

Consciousness is not a system; it has no boundary. Only a system is bounded, but in trying to calibrate yourself and your energy to the way, it takes you an eternity for there exist an infinite number of unique internal qualities surfacing for evaluation, unfolding those qualities, you remain happily in awareness and are never bored, so you simply revolve the energy around that which you have awakened. Now in the physical world, if one side knows not only its awareness but also that of the other, it can calibrate the overall vision for the external fields, which determines what all in that field will see. However, that vision is no guiding light that unites the collective for your internal alarm is alerting you of trouble, but fear can tamper you down, making it difficult to move away from the false vision being propagated.

Those who fracture you, not to mislead you to hope, not to mislead you towards deliverance from external powers, but to awaken and allow your own intelligence to flourish and to flow, on your arrival, a deep sense of gratitude overcomes you for such people. For you realize that the kingdom is really within, no external god is coming to save you and the presence of the Ultimate is always near, you simply needed to be calibrated to align to the way. Calibration brings about an understanding that allows clarity to consume you. Once consumed by clarity, for a moment you feel non-existent, you are now a presence and are one with existence. To be one with existence is not to be fixed but to abide in the clarity of truth, of reality, a dissolution.

Dissolution is psychological fluidity, and anything you fluidize, you stand on, for all fluidization is a window to a greater happening, a greater understanding, thus you stand on it as it unfolds. Being able to stand on it, you can now go with it, with no worries as it leads you. On the contrary, anything that fluidizes you, anything that alters you, destroys you. Consciousness living in clarity, calibrating yourself to consciousness, implies that the energy will always unfold and reveal its profound nature provided you remain a watcher. As you remain a watcher, memory begins to form.

Memory has a direct correlation with time, it is a result of coding crashing energy geometries and storing them. Each location in space has specific memories tied to specific environments. Using local memory protects the local bodies and supports all the minds in that field. Memory must not be too long or too old, or else it kills consciousness. The energy intensifies. Memory is such that when it extends over long periods of time, it becomes destructive. The energy has to crash for higher awareness to bring the higher order. Order is not something fixed.

Take the sun, every revolution around the sun, in a way is a crash of the energy function and an unfoldment of consciousness awareness, a higher order. Anything that propagates old memory through time, its demise will be abrupt for the accumulation cannot continue to sustain and support life. A revolution is precisely to kill the old memories, to kill time, to remain free. Anything linear, such as our construct of time, or our religious books, in a revolution they collapse into a sort of distortion as they try to move with time.

In a revolution, though distorted, consciousness can decode the path of the old, like a camera frame matching the speed of a helicopter propeller, it is an escape velocity. Because of memory, you live in time, the farther back the memory, the harder it is to escape the trappings of time. The point of life is not to be trapped by memory nor to live in memory, this is why life flows, that which flows cannot live in memory for its true purpose is to uncover, to unfold, it has immense energy behind it, the energy of the here and now. With immense energy, to be trapped in memory is disastrous.

Life is not only pulling on you but is also pushing on you and it becomes impossible not to have guilt when living in memory, just drop the memories, for some places you've been having some lows as well as some highs and some moments have been painful and others blissful. This is life, to live, to learn, and to transcend. Not to judge or be a judge.

You have to calibrate the duality instead of allowing the duality to calibrate you. A natural control in nature is simply a gradient, and that which flows above that gradient control is that which sustains life. The river simply follows the course based on subtle gradients that seem invisible, yet all life in the river comes alive. When the control is seen, life is lived in fear, the type of fear that makes you lose everything, and in time, life is extinguished. I am reminded of the Myth of Sisyphus, with the visible up-sloping gradient upon which the boulder is pushed.

This is what's meant by when the control is seen, life is lived in fear. Of course, in the beginning you think it is surmountable, slowly with time you learn what is meant by the control being the failure mode, being the impasse and putting you in a tailspin. When you apply existential nature to a problem, controls are born and control simply divides the flow, it attempts to divide your consciousness, and soon you reach a dead end. It works both ways, for the narcissists who seek to impose on you and for you as you seek to respond and in doing so you create unnecessary controls which shut you down. Yes, controls are necessary, but they have their limits and when too many controls are present, consciousness dies, and equilibrium is lost. Those who impose infinite controls not only get on your nerves, but now you also work against yourself as you seek to create counter-controls. You cannot have it both ways, you can either have controls which kills flow, or you can have consciousness awareness which promotes life and vitality.

We are all plugged into the control of culture which puts us unknowingly on a merry-go-round. On a merry-go-round, you lose touch with reality thus you lose yourself. Losing touch with yourself, you become static, you become robotic and nothing robotic or static can feel. As such the felt presence of the moment escapes you for it is a function of fluidity, the fluidity which unfolds your consciousness awareness. Fluidity allows you to sense all, being able to sense all, equilibrium is maintained and restored, and life is rejuvenated.

You, the consciousness in physical reality, live on a bridge, a rudderless ship guided by all your senses. This is what allows the dance and the unfolding of the intelligence. One end of the bridge is plugged into the energy and the other is plugged into the consciousness awareness. Now science is attempting to replicate this intelligence through what is called artificial intelligence (A.I). A.I is a control in the positive sense for it is only an interlock, a blocker, and flow is negative by nature. How can you interlock ships that are rudderless without some future catastrophic event? When the interlock fractures your ship, you are shipwrecked, and permanently grounded. Those who love you are far gone as their ship continues sailing, even if you are near, you are far apart for they have dreams, goals, and aspirations to attain. Soon you will be separated, and this divide, this duality is the storm of storms destroys the best of minds. Each shipwreck has its own problem even though the storm is the same. Yes, your parents may help you but how can they? They cannot get off their ship to assess you. No one can, not even experts.

Know that when you do something with the heart, that which is easy blesses you. When you do something with logic, that which is easy destroys you, and when done via consciousness awareness both the blessing and the destruction are transcended. When the marginal cost of computing goes to zero as predicted, and A.I becomes the norm, humanity will suffer consequences unknown to man. This will be a collective suffering, a true ugliness. That which is made ugly requires much for it to remain alive and humanity does not have the patience to withstand its own doing, its own positive creation. Who will support you when you are shipwrecked, apart from your mother and father risking their own lives? Who will drop their dreams to help support you? You have to see the truth as it is presented.

Most people feel they are going nowhere, and it is because we tend to live on the surface, towards superficiality and thus have become superficial. You are conditioned to have surface values while your ship requires depth for it to sail, to not run aground, and it requires depth so you can navigate. You have to steer your own ship, for only you can have a feel for it, for no one else senses your conscious reality. True intelligence is a function of freedom, while artificial intelligence is a function of patterns, and boundaries, thus AI can never gain true intelligence for it lacks the quality of being. Quality of being is a function of the likes of Buddha, Lao Tzu, Osho, Ogou, and Christ like consciousness'. In thinking of the nature of the Buddha, Ogou, Jesus, and Lao Tzu, you learn that you if you do not awaken, you cannot want nor can you possess the quality of something whose energy you didn't seek to understand. Energy crashes and consciousness unfolds, and through that unfoldment process, it has the potential to awaken.

Music works this way, physical love works this way, nature works this way, and even our food is grown this way. You can play with the light, but you must know that you are inducing hell, you have to understand the light and its limitations. The light shines for all so none have to illuminate your path and trap you. The real pain is realizing you're being pulled apart at the speed of thinking. A true desert land with no ability to ever become whole. Imagine having a reboiler in the middle of the ocean, this is a metaphor of course but it is an important one. A reboiler in the ocean, what gets destroyed first is ocean life, your qualities, and never to come back. What goes next is steam visible by all, and you can call that behavior issues as it is manifested.

Any impact on form or body destroys your ability to become spiritual nor does it allow you to see any quality from the spiritual. The meaning of spiritual here must be understood as the word has been poisoned by culture through time. Traditional religions do not teach nor demonstrate spirituality in its true essence, they are concerned with rituals and symbology, not reality nor divinity.

## Chapter 5

## The Foundation Beyond Time

You have probably noticed that nothing written in this book conveys the depth of the vibration from which existence speaks through you, and the depth is so deep that you wonder if anyone else sees the reality the way you do. With this minimal ability, I will attempt to try to understand this digital era we live in that has made us all egotistical in nature and, at the same time, divided society where, to some, it has become meaningless. The problem with the digital era is that it will fracture all material in form, including you. It will discover all secrets, but these discoveries are not to help you—they are to push the mind to interact with the two vanishing points, a condition that will be difficult to move away from. Once such knowledge and technologies come against you, you are fighting yourself, you are fighting all the intelligent minds that have contributed to science over centuries.

To fight yourself is to imprison yourself and the only way out is to resist everything that seeks to impose on you, allowing you to induce and awaken your intelligence and, at the same time, fight with nothing external to you. Everything in the external environment is of greater inductive nature and has come from greater field sources capable of destroying your gracefulness. To resist everything is to drop their energy as they seek to push and impinge on the mind, not to physically fight and resist. This allows you to move away from the destructive energy of the mind. Everything in form is mind as such. You can either seek to understand, and through that understanding, you cancel the energy, or you can allow the energy to impinge on you, which, in time, moves you towards distinction.

In modern culture, society has reached a point where the science not only penetrates all aspects of our doing, but it also permeates all aspects and functions of our lives. You have to see that humanity wants science without borders, meaning the ability to destroy with impunity, to be intrusive without any permission or any repercussion. You have to hand it to the scientists… they have found some great discoveries and have managed to create and bring comfort to humanity that is second to none. They have done such a good job that the marginal cost of energy and computing has been reduced to almost nothing—zero, you can say. The marginal cost of energy and computing being zero is science without borders, a focused hell unleashed on humanity. Osho tells us that science is "knowledge without love", and you only have to see the historical patterns of wars that the planet has suffered and endured to see where science without borders is taking humanity. Including religious wars, that which should have freed you and brought you to a quality state of mind, yet have only enslaved you.

To have a true future, science needs to know its boundaries, to not apply its methods to the "inner being", and religions need to be morphed to religiousness where individual godliness permeates society. Both science and religion need to be transcended. Science has become a hell that seeks only destruction and religion seeks to raise hell when you question their foundations, which trap your psychology with dogmas. When you get lost in the foundation, you cannot realize the essence of the Ultimate, what Jesus called the realization of the kingdom within.

Though energy is the foundation, and though it goes on crashing each solar cycle, the consciousness in man never evolves. It never unfolds to its true potential. It remains repressed and that repression is like a quicksand that slowly entrenches humanity in chaos and the propagation of chaos. Some ask for solutions and no solution will be a quick fix. Meditation is the only tool that awakens you to your internal chaos. Nobody likes chaos yet we have become accustomed to the chaotic nature of life—it has become second nature. As such, everything is propagated at speeds beyond your ability to understand the concerns and their impact to your foundation.

A foundation is the past, the past is held together via a vanishing point that is intense and unknown. To interact with the vanishing point from the past is to kill the future. To interact with the vanishing point from the past in the here and now is to kill both the future and waste time in a focal point whose exit output could not have known the input. I hear some talking about how, when a family member dies, they will see that person again. This is absolutely false. How can you, being consciousness and not form, who live independent of coordinates, who live beyond any foundation, think that when you die you will see those from the past? This cannot be true, if so then consciousness is false, it is non-foundational, yet we know that nothing exists without consciousness awareness and not a single person can deny their own personal consciousness and how it evolves and unfolds.

As a result of memory, we imagine an afterlife where we will see all our ancestors because our families are dear to us, the memories we create together build the foundation that gives us stability and creates joy within.

All is within, nothing exists out there, and if we create fantasies, they become gaps in the foundation. To think of all the beings that will accumulate in the afterlife creates the same problem we have on this planet—that of accumulation. Such accumulation and impingement of minds would create tremendous discomfort that destroys the urge to see them. Worshiping your ancestors is the same as when you wake up and enjoy the sun in a meditative way. The tingling on your skin is their presence. We worship ancestors because we can never go back in time, yet they are the light that guides, and humanity has a common ancestry, irrespective of our divides, for the sun shines for all and our consciousness' are indivisible.

You have to remember, the past has weight, therefore, it is dead. The future is weightless; therefore, it is alive, and only that which is alive can love and all love comes from the here and now, the indivisible whole, consciousness, that which is never born and never dies. Who can fall in love with a thing, with a past that weighs you down? Drop the past, you are consciousness, you can go nowhere, nor can you ever go back in time when you die because you do not live in time, and bodies exist only in time. Some talk of a reset in the here and now, and I wonder how one can talk of a reset when the composition of the vanishing point from the past is unknown, and to interact with it is to invert life and bring about destruction.

Only consciousness has the awareness to free you from the past, to discard its weight and to bring you to the present. Therefore, God is not external to you, for anything external is duality. Religion means to unite and bring all the parts together but all they have come to be in time are tools of division. There cannot be different religions. To say different religions exists it is to destroy the meaning of the word and, at the same time, stating that there exists different consciousness. If meaning comes from that which is centered on wholeness, which gives us understanding and religiousness, then spirituality is crucial. There is only one consciousness common to all of humanity. Move closer towards Zen and transcend both science and religion where your spirituality becomes your essence. Zen meditation stands above both science and religion because the two-headed monsters are partial—they are partial foundations that unleash hell.

Your consciousness cannot be trapped in foundations for that fixes your position, you have to mature, you have to see the inner being, the inner spirit, your true self, and move away from duality of mind. Yes, duality is a fracturing force, and you have to remember that a fracturing force has no value after having fractured all, therefore, the fractured equally have no value. Do not seek to fight with a force capable of fracturing and destroying you. At the same time, you cannot allow it to destroy you either as that means you are an enabler of destruction, a follower of patterns, a seed which propagates destruction.

Find a way to create a boundary, something that can give you some shade from such destructive forces. All value depends on the boundary layer between the fracturing force and the life-giving force able to maintain interconnectedness, bridged together below by fields from top to bottom. Thus, that which becomes a tool is valueless in the grand scheme, its value is derived on how much you can get for it. It is this psychology that is destroying the planet. You cannot allow a tool that is distinct by nature to turn you into a tool, for a tool is an object that never changes, and dealing with that which does not change diminishes your highest value, it diminishes your consciousness, it destroys your quality within, and as such, you become a piece of furniture. Know that values only come from consciousness and not that which fractures for only consciousness is able to see, only consciousness can have intelligence as it is your consciousness that allows you to move away from mind.

When conscious entities are trapped in foundations such as books, which are outdated, or anything fixed propagated through time, they become dangerous, they become violent, for everything of quality is found beyond their structure in the here and now. Anything of quality will always be contemporary and contemporary is a result of not being intrusive. True contemporary will never be intrusive, it always live intemporaneously.

To live intemporaneously is to live in the here and now, and when you become fixed and planted, your consciousness is trapped in foundations and you have lost your freedom. Freedom allows you to explore, and when you explore the depth of your consciousness, all your qualities spring forward. Meditation moves you away from the old mind that was destroying you, the negative culture you created. Religions create foundational dogmas so they can be fixed, and science have to take things apart so they can be understood, the former attempting to fix your position and the latter to take you apart. In such environment, what hope can there be for life when you are bounded by religions and science without borders seeking to plant and fix you? All the religious institutions cannot see everything beyond their foundations, they can sense the beauty beyond, they can see the quality, yet they can only watch while the house gets built. They are split between what they have dug up and the beauty that escapes them, angering themselves, they live in distress as they watch existence unfold. There is tremendous beauty in life when understood from the cosmic order, when we can see that most problems are our own making.

Most institutions function that way, including all the major religions. They see everything but they are simply in a foundational role, trapped in a condition with dogmas that cannot stand the test of time. Religious dogmas are the psychological foundations of most people on this planet. Their concept of the universe comes from these religious doctrines, which contradicts the scientific understanding of the universe as proposed by some theories. You have to know that you cannot have foundational religious dogmas that contradict science, for religion is of "Truth" and science must not contradict truth for there is only one truth.

You have to build the house to know what it is like to be at home, and to know that the foundation is not the house. You have to understand the mind and what it is to move towards no mind in order to know your qualities. Yes, it will be difficult to build, it will take time, and there will be mistakes and errors. You cannot be like most people—those who sleep on foundations thinking that it is the house. Most people are sleeping on foundations, trapped in logic, which is why so much hell is unleashed on the world. You cannot have the foundation, your life energy, that which crashes with each cycle be the roof of the house and expect a stable house and a stable environment. Doing so, you are always collapsing your culture, always creating narratives and putting your life at risk. You will inevitably collapse the whole house at some point in time.

Can't you see that anything you cut and plant back in the foundation will always yield the same pattern—something dead? A pattern is a dead thing. In the book, "I am the Gate", Osho calls the phenomenal plane, constant surface level changes. A human being is not something to be planted, by doing so, the being in you dies. You are not a thing, you are human, a conscious being. You have to see that humanity has been dying for a long time, but you do not see it based on your concept of time. When you are using words derived from the objective reality to describe the divine, and insisting they are truth, you can only get trapped.

Most foundational dogmatic institutions have not a sense of truth. How can they be of truth when truth comes from realized beings? Those who can bring cosmic understanding to a focal point for the understanding of life itself. When you bring cosmic understanding to a focal point, objectivity disappears, and to bind understanding with narratives of old, you are wielding a sword, you are seeking destruction. Do not try to make foundational dogmatic words your roof, for you can never approach the real with dogmatic understanding, as such, you remain trapped and immature. When you bring cosmic understanding to a focal point and bind it with silence, you are awakening all life, you are uniting the collective divinity through the joy of the heart intelligence that flows through all of humanity.

Life flows and its true methods are unknown and will remain unknown so that your heart remains open to love, to truth, and to the future. You have to see that when something becomes knowledge, when something becomes known, the mind closes the heart, and death and decay prevails in the phenomenal plane. With this, you can easily see that love is not a function of power but of freedom and understanding. Power is intense and it binds you to where you can have no intelligence. Intelligence comes only from cosmic love. That which is intense creates an invisible path, for intensity is a portal and consciousness does not function with intensity. Intensity keeps you tense and consciousness awareness relaxes you. Know that the mind can only see that which lies at the edge of an intense existence or an intense happening, as such, this seeing is surface level—it lacks the depth from which understanding unfolds.

Anything that is dead, whether objects, words, or religion, their intensity in the here and now becomes a sort of fusion that destroys life. They add weight to the psychology of the individual, blocking the path to enlightenment. Uniting consciousness expands the portal to the life source unknown to us and invites greater possibilities from the divine light of existence. The mind, no matter how powerful, can only explore the boundaries of life, therefore, we get trapped in the superficial, we get trapped in the past, and we get trapped in form and ignore the real. We ignore the silence out of which existence quietly opens its gates. The mind, given all its powers, can only function in duality. It can only see black and white. Seeing black and white is computation, ones and zeros which are functions of the mind and not of consciousness.

You, being consciousness, no words can describe you, no foundations can know you. Neti, neti. Humanity never had a chance to truly evolve in the cosmic sense, for the narratives we carry through time become mental constraints that are difficult to overcome. Narratives that are difficult to drop, hence the sword is bloody, your hands are dirty, and it becomes difficult to wash your hands, for to do so, you will be exposed. You are afraid of saying that you do not know.

Zen is not a narrative, it flows through you from higher orders to higher orders. How can you attempt to grasp something far beyond the mind and bind it with words? It is not possible, the scientific method cannot be applicable to the inner understanding of consciousness, yet science is moving towards the same foundational errors done by religions, and if science becomes a foundation, that which takes things apart, what hope is there for humanity? It is you that has to move towards the foundation when you want to, but if the foundation comes to you and imposes on you, you are in hell. You, being consciousness in form, when you go to your foundation for wisdom, it burns off your concerns, moving you to clarity. You can call that a type of sunbathing—an undeniable interchange of felt presence.

All concerns and all the problems of men and women are a lack of natural flow, and when a foundation restricts flow, it is false. Can the sun rays never not reach you so long as you are alive? Though they go through you daily, with no thought to you of their presence as you bask in comfort, and even more unpronounced than solar rays flowing through you is your consciousness that escapes your awareness and that too goes completely unnoticed.

Dogmatic institutions, being foundations, used to be a reliable source but are now inverting. Remember, a foundation is common to all and partial to none. Hence the sun, and when you return to the understanding of your foundation to solve problems, none of the images you have constructed can be found there, it is only a sunbathing in clarity, pure sensing and awareness. In the presence of your foundation, you have to drop all concept in time, you have to drop all fears and enter into silence as the awareness illuminates you. What behavior can you assign to such nature of stillness, a form of download? Who has gone to the beach and has not felt such a pure sense of being—an unexpressed deep thankfulness for the light of being? No one can deny this attunement to our true foundation.

We are so busy trapping the future in the past that we cannot see the fact that our true foundation has no sense of history. Yes, your memory is historical but your true foundation cannot be historical. If you try to impose a sense of history on your foundation, you bring it on you, you invite your own destruction, the cycle of the energy cannot turn, and in the process, the energy comes under great pressure. Any time one senses intense pressure, fear is present, and as such, you naturally gravitate towards an attachment. When one gravitates toward an attachment because of fear, your attachment or the relationship with the attached cannot be called love. Love is beyond the limits of the mind and is a product of consciousness expansion, thus it remains a mystery.

All attachments are prisons and are against life. Attachments are functions of not only fear but also ego, and Krishnamurti taught us that to fear is to be violent. You can easily see that those who function with the ego are violent individuals. This is why most people are against egos. The egotistical exhibit a violent under tone—they are sadist and masochist. Yes, the ego has to die but it does not mean to kill it completely. To kill the ego in the conscious sense is to bring it to Yoga, and to bring it to Yoga is what Patanjali calls "you, controlling the rising of the mind into ripples." Some ego is a necessity for ego is a vector, and vectors allow you to travel paths.

To travel a path in life, there has to be some sort of a fracture, allowing you to find your way, yet you have to understand the nature of existence and its source. This understanding allows you to see that in order for a pathway to exist, there has to be a form of Yogic egoism capable of seeing the rise of the ripples, capable of uniting the divide, and being capable of replicating itself and birthing the path for the continuation of conscious evaluation without destroying the nature of that which is. The inability to understand reality and the absolute will bound you by that which destroys you.

The first boundary that becomes destructive when misaligned is thought, beginning with individual thought, followed by that of the group. Group thinking or dogmatic thinking are the most destructive forms of psychological thinking. The moment collective thinking becomes destructive, the actions and creations of this group generates greater means of destructive layers. Religion cannot save humanity, for religions as they exist today are not only dogmatic but are primitive and misleading. Meditation, capable of bringing humanity to discover their spirituality and religiousness, is the only method that can give man the courage needed to go beyond the destructive unconscious foundational layers of mind. Meditation moves you towards religiousness and religiousness is fluid while religion is rigid. Religiousness is a flow state capable of drawing the best out of you with each turn life takes—this is real education. Religion is dogma. It cannot offer you anything more than its nature of the symbolic. Religion deals with power and power can only imprison, whether be it those who hold the power or those it seeks to rule using such power. This is the ugliest form of ego, that which generates fear.

The need to constantly differentiate and always be stimulated hinders your ability to be one with yourself as you get trapped in differential analysis. Differentiation is a great divide that has been misunderstood, and in truth, differences are an opening. The divide can be due to either stimulus response or many other causes. Your continuation of accumulating differences over time shifts you towards a mode of functioning that prevents you from seeing truth and being with the Real. You now function only in time—both physically and psychologically.

It is important to understand what is meant by functioning in time physically. This functioning is a natural phenomenon, your body grows in time, your mind develops through time, and all physical growth in the environment is what is meant by functioning in physical time. To function with psychological time, you destroy your sanity. This is what is called a constant grind—a state that wears you down at an unimaginable rate. With psychology that functions in time, nothing is appreciated, nothing is cared for as you only look to find utility in everything. The clarity obtained from differentiation has to lead you to a non-differentiable state of being, turning the mind inwards towards introspection, birthing greater consciousness awareness. The more you practice this, you are normalizing around wholeness. Having moved towards a non-differentiable state of being, all is appreciated, you recognize that all is an integral part of the manifestation of the whole. This recognition moves you away from emptiness to spaciousness, to recognize the natural occurrences and not those that are manmade, nor those forced via coercive actions by humanity, which tend to deceive in order to move you towards a position contrary to your understanding.

Differentiation is double-edged, to be double-edged is to know there is a positive and a negative function. You have to know that most people function on the negative aspect of the difference, hence the need to understand natural versus that which can deceive. They come packaged together as humanity's logic is deceptive. In cultural terms, negative is associated with something not palatable for society and positive as palatable. This duality destroys the understanding of reality.

To understand reality, you will need to understand context and not sound bites, for meaning cannot be conveyed through sound bites. In existence, the negative implies the ability to flow, and the positive is a blocker, a stone, a rock. These minute differences are necessary to understand to not be in your own way. Constant stimulus response erodes consciousness, and over time, you are no longer a human being. Simply a robot—a tool. Adults are no longer adults in the sense they can take responsibility but are waiting for the next opportunity to be stimulated. This mode of living hides from you all qualities that existence endowed you and offered you.

Stimulus response has a greater ability to destroy. It has the capability to apply a greater force, hence its ability to destroy all that becomes addictive. Consciousness awareness, on the other hand, illuminates patterns for analysis, whether addictive or not, enabling you to transcend. The question to ask is, do you see your self-importance tied to your self-image as a process, or is it some static fixed image? If you see it as a process, you embrace all seasons, for the energy must crash, and the beauty of Existence and grace is manifested as it must, not as you would like. If you see it as a static final image, then self-conflict arises, for the ego is confused in the summer, fall, winter, and spring. In confusion, intelligence cannot flow.

You have to be careful with external images driving you to action, for the image is not the real thing and the conditions leading someone to a specific place and action are not and will not be the same for you. You have a different internal flow state to each and every one and everything around you. You may be disappointed trying to follow someone and moving to action based on a projected image as they can lead you to your downfall unexpectedly. It is best to be still until the right action presents itself. Understand the background first, then remove compulsion and emotion and see how you thrive and become peaceful. Often, you are moved by an image presented to you, yet you have no understanding of the background, and there are potential dangers embedded in said image or idea. For example, you can't marry a girl without marrying her entire family, for they have formulated her mind since birth. Meaning, unless an individual has awakened to their conditioning and discover their true self, they will have flaws that you will have to be patient in helping them work through.

My parents tell a beautiful story of their separation when my mother was pregnant with me. In the first trimester of the pregnancy, my father's family intervened and prevented him from being with my mother. They thought there were other women better suited for him. They hid him from my mom all throughout her pregnancy. She gave birth without his presence and had to go through ridicule from her family because they were against their union from the beginning. A few weeks after I was born, my father came to his senses and ditched his family to join who would be his future wife now of fifty years. You can see how even your own family members can have a complete disregard for your well-being. Everybody wants to control you, to tell you what to do. It is not their fault for they do not know who they are. You have to know from the heart whether a decision will bring you a stable outcome and whether it will continue moving you towards greater stability. Both my parents discarded the image that their parents wanted for each of them and charted their own course.

When at a difficult crossroad, you have to ask yourself if that is what you want to be a part of. Instead of trying to patch an emotional emptiness, which will persist if the wrong decision is made, discern wisely. People's intentions around you reveal their character no matter how nice they may seem, and it takes courage to transcend one's thinking and thought processes to move towards what is good for you as this requires lifting the mask we all hide behind. You must not be afraid. Whatever you're not afraid of, that is the way—anything you are afraid of is not the way. If you're not afraid to be free, then freedom is the way, if you're not afraid to love, then love is the way, if you're not afraid to destroy, then destruction is the way. Anything you're afraid of cannot be the way for it puts a lid on the mind and pressurizes you in subtle ways and destroys you in time. I'm not afraid to leave dogmatic religion in order to meditate for dogmatic religion is not the way, they do not live up to the meaning of the word. I am not afraid to follow Zen, for Zen is the way. Zen is freedom, and without freedom, you cannot love. Without freedom, you cannot be, and if you cannot love and cannot be, then what is life? Zen is the ultimate freedom. Zen puts no boundaries on your sense of being, Zen takes you beyond mind and beyond form. Remember, "You cannot get nourishment in a world where you are a slave," everybody wants to own you and wants to tell you what to do, Drop the past.

The Cosmic Candle

# Chapter 6

## The Veil of Psychological Time

Conditioning is the greatest barrier to seeing how your ego misleads you and creates so many problems. Most of us are linear thinkers and one must ask oneself, what is linear thought and linear thinking? You see, linear thought and thinking is being so engulfed in the outcome that one ignores all the immediate things that are happening in your surroundings that impinge to push you astray. Like having a straight line between you and the end goal. Having such a line of thinking is dangerous in a multi-variate world, and the inability to see the shift in your surroundings will blind you to the necessary conditions needed for meeting your goal. Thus, to transcend linear thought is to completely disassociate oneself with expectations, outcomes, and to be aware in the present moment.

You need to be aware of your mental processes and ask yourself, how does one transcend linear thought? To do so requires you to focus on your actions leading to the desired goal. All actions create pathways in the brain that if the consequences are favorable, one is likely to repeat those actions, and if unfavorable, the subsequent action is modified by the individual thereby gaining knowledge of what is appropriate or inappropriate action. You see, what you know fixes your position and something becomes knowledge upon the confirmation of the fact. Given these two points of understanding, the ability to know internal states implies the ability to manipulate physical reality but for a short time only, for to manipulate physical reality in a greater time frame is the greatest manifestation of ego. This will wear off and all the unseen gaps created in the process will come back and be closed in the worse ways.

Look at the era we are living in and how men address their affairs. Only through Transcendence are you able to minimize actions, attenuate knowledge, and become consciously aware of them. You have to become completely aware of every thought and action, for only once aware can one align the necessary conditions to lead to a desired consequence. You see, all thoughts and actions lead to consequences that are either favorable or unfavorable. The key lies in identifying the pathways or actions that lead to unfavorable conditions and iterating them until alignment away from such conditions are achieved. The problem is that most people want to dissociate themselves from the unfavorable outcomes or completely absolve themselves from their negative actions when they should be taking responsibility. In the education of humanity, everyone that has been through formal education is like a rattlesnake harboring the poisons of ideology from their local habitat—they do not know who they are themselves. The focus subject from their education determines what's concentrated within. Where each level in education conditions the student to a time that leaves a residue on the mind that brings internal conflict in the here and now, the shedding of the subsequent layers of skin, which, in time, becomes the rattle serving as a warning tool.

As one moves away from the lower levels towards higher levels, you are unaware of their dangers and their effects. Every year, you move on to the next level and think you've gained knowledge. You think you have gained understanding, yet you have simply been conditioned. Each year, the potency of that within amasses, the potency strengthens, and by the time one graduates, you have become a tool.

When you are educated by a third party, you think you are significant and above all. You must never use your significance to climb the ladder of self-importance, this is ugly, sending unwanted vibrations. When someone tells you to leave it up to God, you have to ask yourself, what is the difference between the common saying, "It is what it is", and leaving it to God? This is fatalism, the seed of irresponsibility—a complete disregard for life and the dignity of life. A pattern is a reference that points to an unseen source, a foundation, hence why it escapes most people. A pattern is a dead thing.

I have observed, walking on trails that, although all trees look similar, non-differential, they all have different patterns. They are unique and not one even in the same species has the same pattern. Men have managed to push false patterns on each other, creating fear in individuals, thus the ability to be one with the divine escapes them. Fear is not true, fear implies a misunderstanding of a phenomenon and you have to do some work to move beyond its impact on the mind given the inductive nature of the mind. The mind is always inclined to think of something missing, of something wrong, creating divisions that push you to move to the next thought, thereby inducing flow.

Flow is a function of the negative, and "the negative is the role of the master to remove the rock so you can flow." The master cannot teach you kindness nor how to be a sage, for that only comes by having transcended duality and only you can transcend your experiences. Osho tells us, "Experience is possible only in duality." Duality is inductive—anything inductive, you have to move beyond it to understand it, hence the quest for no mind. All is shown to us in nature, it is matter of recognizing the truth. Truth comes only from nature, familiarize your mind with nature and not the creation of man. Just as we live far from the inductive nature of the sun, position perfectly to move with truth, the nature of cosmic order. You, the consciousness in you, lives beyond the mind but localized in mind as a bridge, your local non-local center. With the mind being inductive, the only way to save yourself if you have gone the wrong route is to bound everything with silence. The late Great Terence McKenna tells us, "Science is inductive," the truth is, the mind is inductive, for it is ever dividing itself and thus cannot have longevity without the integrative function of consciousness awareness. Yet you'll find that when you let go of mind, all is there, all wants to present itself, it bubbles to the surface.

When you understand that the mind is inductive, you are careful of the seeds you plant. Meaning, when you plant the correct seed, they cannot but grow to provide shade. Just like kindness cannot but expand to yield goodness. This is not the pseudo-subservient kindness with ill intentions but one of dignity, struggles, and gracefulness. This kindness asks for nothing and begs for nothing. Anything that is inductive cannot be true for its accumulation contains many parts whose integrative geometry are beyond the nature of your psychic receptivity to understand, and thus do not belong to you. It does not mean the inductive is meaningless and devoid of constructive functions, just that your perception of the inductive is false. Now you may wonder, why is something that is inductive false? It is false for there exists an infinite number of potential paths once the fracture of the mind occurs. The path of the fracture cannot be known to you as the accumulation of new geometrical configurations propagates through time. These occurrences are nature's assurance of the uniqueness of all things in existence, therefore, nothing can ever be a duplicate for that reason. This also is fractal in nature, from the smallest object to the biggest, as well as from the smallest planet to the biggest. Without the ability to propagate uniqueness, you become fixed and thus decay. Anything fixed, propagated through time, eventually collapses or else it destroys all around it. This also applies to humans and their psychology.

There is a saying Osho tell us, "It is not enough to save the next generation from wars if they are simply carbon copies of you. What is the point? If they are carbon copies of you, they will do the same as you have been doing. A new man is needed. A new man who feels the whole earth his mother, not small segments. Do you see, you call your land the mother land, and you have cut the mother in so many pieces." You are supposed to be that which sees that which transcends duality, or else you become destructive. You cannot torture mother earth through false science, divide her into differences brought against each other and not expect a war-like atmosphere. You have to be able to see that an inductive body by itself is the worst form of destruction. Inductive bodies have to revolve around other inductive bodies in tune with existence for stability to resound. Just look at the stars you'll see, the sky is full of stars and not just one. Hence the dangers of isolation.

Anything alone or anything functioning only one way will be destructive, and for that reason, you have to see that consciousness is not a way, it is life itself—the Absolute. Hence, on earth, consciousness is the truth propagating itself, never dual, the male and female energy being the vehicle of propagating local consciousness in form. This is why religions and dogmas accustomed by society are dangerous. They are dualistic and not of truth. Science is incomplete and will always be incomplete, and the source of induction is truth yet that which is inductive cannot itself be true. Though that which is inductive may not be true, its collective functioning seeks truth and not dogmas.

Chapter 7

Psychological States of Awareness

The rhythm of the ocean is marvelous, for it is in perfect harmony with the winds of time. This is the state of being we are all searching for in this life. To be in perfect harmony with yourself is—a state that cannot be grasped with a cluttered mind—to be free, to be fluid in thought, to be fluid in motion, to be fluid in understanding, but most importantly, to seek conceptual boundary expansion. Standing on the shores of the ocean, the vastness and spaciousness evokes your awareness of that which lies beyond, you cannot name it, you cannot put your finger on it, yet the presence is felt. Standing on the shore, the vastness of existence pulls on you to look within, for the felt presence unfolds your essence. When felt presence unfolds your essence, you are weightless, you are like the wind, your dance becomes existential, it becomes an oceanic feel. Essence kindles the type of understanding that is unique to your being, this understanding is a gradient of cosmic order, that which is not based on desire or ego.

Life has gotten so difficult that the burdens are heavy, everyone in society is carrying a heaviness that leaves them feeling empty. You must understand the word emptiness, for there exists the emptiness that evokes the vastness of existence, often referred to as a nothingness by mystics, and the emptiness brought about by the burdens from daily living, the burdens from your lack of depth and the emptiness felt within when you are alone as you are afraid to face yourself. Emptiness is defined as a state of containing nothing, the quality of lacking meaning. It is easy to see that when you lack meaning, your life is quickly filled with burdens, you feel lost. As such, I have developed a psychological model of moving you away from meaninglessness, what I consider going from a puddle to a pond, a pond to a lake, a lake to an ocean, and an ocean to authentic existentialism. These models are for you to become consciously aware of the limitations of your psychic receptivity as they are now, as well as your potential at each level as you expand your consciousness awareness. Overcoming these limitations is the beginning of enlightenment. Enlightenment is not what most people think, and meditation is also not what most people think. Societal conditioning of the mind creates a fear in you that keeps you from moving towards meditation, that keeps you from moving towards truth, and that keeps you from accepting your solitude and your aloneness. Meditation is great fun and is a tremendous unfoldment of beauty, enough to move you away from any negativity.

The first psychological state is that of a puddle, and as a puddle, you are bound and limited. Meaninglessness becomes the vehicle to hopelessness, you easily destroy yourself, you lack depth, and everything becomes a burden and a nuisance to your being. In this psychological state, external events being out of your control limit your range of motion, resulting in felt pain. All the pain, all the feelings of pain, all the feelings of emptiness brought about by burdens are difficult on your being as your sense of emptiness is so burdensome and so heavy that it is easily overpowered by other substance of greater value, it leaves you feeling helpless and powerless. The feeling of emptiness, brought about by burdens, is the reason you seek power, for power is explosive, power is destructive, and when you are powerful, you use such power to overcome that which seeks to impose on you, becoming destructive to yourself. This, I call functioning with a puddle psychology the state to move away from on the journey to higher consciousness awareness.

The nature of puddle psychology is such that you cannot see beyond your fears. You cannot see that your search for power cannot be encompassed in your puddle psychology, the inadequate space you currently occupy. This is double jeopardy in a way, your need for a false desire and your fear of being found out of your own inadequacy. You can fix this, you can remove the clutter without feeling the inadequacy, without the need for the will to power, but first, you have to be willing to accept your ignorance, to accept your cultural conditioning, and resolve the negative consequences brought about as a result of such conditioning. Culture is a subtle form of control, and the moment control comes into being, hierarchy also comes into being as a form of constraint and begins to multiply. See for yourself, all hierarchical structures are to ensure the right level of competence are present in any system and are themselves at each level potential failure modes that weigh on the system, thus are themselves additional constraints. It is the compounding of constraints that gives you the feeling of emptiness, the feeling and the sense of powerless. Yes, the feeling is heavy, it seems hopeless, and any time hopelessness is present, you want to drop your responsibility, you want to be entertained, you need stimulants, and soon, this becomes your norm, this becomes your normal psychology and you remain stuck in a puddle.

The second psychological state is that of a pond. In this state of consciousness, you expand your psychological awareness into that of the pond, you have developed some depth through the recognition that power does not solve problems. That simple recognition by itself is enough to move you in the right direction, to get you to see things in degrees. All that is needed to see things in degrees is the awareness that you are not an object, you are not fixed into position, you have an axial view of this phenomenal reality. A simple turnaround from a false desire is enough to get you going. This small step is enough to fracture and move you towards the pond. As you move towards the pond, your perception increases, you expand your cognitive abilities and gain awareness of your own nature. It is your nature that has you moving towards the false desires and the negative aspects cluttering your mind. As you move closer towards the pond, as you remove clutter and gain depth, this is getting you to see the futility of the quest for power, the futility of the quest for self-importance, and in this psychological state, you have gained awareness that your boundary can be expanded to include better quality information.

The spark of psychological evolution is now triggered, the possibilities of evolution and the ability to unfold higher consciousness awareness is bubbling within you. In this state of awareness, for the first time, you understand the meaning of fragility, you understand that events can drain you and destroy you, but you have become more resistant to nuances and certain pressures. Now you know the pond is not the goal, you know a simple shift cannot be all there is, you can feel the gradient pull is too strong for the pond to be the end goal. In the pond, you can see the dirty water—an indication that it is not the goal. This dirtiness is your own making, it is you throwing off the burdens. But now you can no longer escape them, you can see them swimming around you, you can see also everything growing in it, and as such, your degrees of freedom are limited. The lack of degrees of freedom are painful, and even through the pain, the gradient pull is strong enough to alert you to still higher states of consciousness awareness, but you are afraid because the pond can be filled with dirt, bringing you back to the puddle psychology. What to do now? This is where meditation comes in, this is where you must move away from the old. This is where enlightenment begins, to take you on the journey to higher consciousness awareness. This is where the journey to the third psychological state of awareness begins—that of the lake.

The third psychological state is that of a lake. Once you can find the strength to go with the awareness pulling on your being, the psychology is developing to what is comparable to a lake. Before, when you were in the pond, you were tired from the constraints, tired of all the discomforts, tired of the lack of degrees of freedom. But this pond is what you know. You have gotten accustomed to being in the pond, and to move away towards an unknown is of greater trepidation, but the pond is too small, and you have to move away from the pond. Between each stage, you will find that it is meditation that removes the fear brought about from the gradient pulling on you. Meditation is your bridge, just as a state of silence is your bridge from moment to moment, even though you are not aware of the silence.

Meditation is the bridge from the lower form of consciousness to the higher form of consciousness. As you begin to move away from the pond, the gradient is no longer so. You have entered into the boundary of the lake and are now exploring depths that eluded you for so long. You are now able to chart your course, you are able to dance a little, and you are able to withstand most pressures of things thrown at you. You begin to understand who you are and how you have created your troubles, and for the first time, you have gained a glimpse of your mind. This glimpse, this seeing, frees you from the objectivity of the mind. You can now pick things up and move them around and watch them sink to their depths. See for yourself, next time you are near a lake, pick up a rock and throw it into the lake, see how it just sinks to the bottom worry-free, becoming invisible to everyone.

These are the joys of higher consciousness awareness that escapes the lower psychological conditioning. In this higher psychological state, you begin to understand the concept of oneness, to understand what it means to be one with creation. You begin to see that the dance between you and the winds of time are starting to synchronize, and each degree gains their equivalence in understanding. Insight is now triggered, and when things are thrown your way, you know how to simply let them go and let them sink to the bottom. Having gained such depth of understanding, the gradient pull is no longer a pull, you are standing on the bridge of awareness, but this bridge no longer points towards the lower states of consciousness. This bridge is the bridge between no mind and that which Osho calls super consciousness and cosmic consciousness. Recognizing you are this bridge is tremendous work, and from this bridge, you will become devoted, and as you gain higher consciousness awareness, you will move on the path towards existentialism.

The fourth psychological state is that of an ocean. As an ocean, your capabilities have expanded beyond any comprehension, and those wanting to destroy you, doing so, will destroy something that serves the common good. In this state of consciousness awareness, you have attained what is often referred to as the oceanic feel where your life becomes a dance with the cosmic one, the cosmic energy, and you entered wholeness with your full being. In this cosmic dance, this awareness of being one with existence unites you with the oceanic feel and the winds of time, the indubitable state of you having arrived. Yes, life can be burdensome as most things in life are beyond your control, but one can free oneself via mental expansion through prayer and meditation. When bigger things are thrown at you, which are meant to destroy you, simply let them sink to the bottom, for the dance is too beautiful to let others disrupt your dance. Your boundaries have gotten so vast that it becomes immeasurable.

When you have reached the oceanic feel, you can call yourself human, for the true unfolding of your consciousness awareness has taken place, and that unfoldment will be of cosmic order. You are now in the middle position as defined by the word meaning of man. You are now the cosmic candle in the sea of darkness. In this state, all of existence supports you and balances you and the energy comes alive. As master Osho says, enlightenment is only the beginning for the vastness of existence is such that nothing can contain, and you will only ever be nothing in this phenomenal plane, only consciousness in form, only a bridge, but the quality of your bridge depends on your awakening.

The fifth psychological state is going from the oceanic state to authentic existentialism. Authentic existentialism is you expanding your bridge of consciousness awareness, oscillating from no mind to super consciousness and cosmic consciousness, using cosmic understanding to incarnate and give back to humanity. Authentic existentialism is the cosmic candle. All the works from the greatest masters come from this psychological state of being. Works from masters the likes of Osho, Khalil Gibran, Mikhail Naimi, Sri Ramana Marshi, etc. These masters and their works transcend time, helping generation after generation. Authentic existentialism is remaining in the oceanic feel, the highest-level awareness from where insight, intuition, and intelligence become one, it is to live in truth. Truth brings you toward the state of no mind at the gates of existence. Truth is boundless for there are no illusions, and the mind requires a boundary for it to maintain its illusions upon which the ego lives. Authentic masters do not work with mind, for working with mind you need wisdom. Working with truth, you need the presence of grace. Gracefulness moves you towards silence, and through silence, you find the thread to undo mind.

# Chapter 8

## Illumination and Consciousness

Any time or anywhere there exists vibration, you will find consciousness, for vibrations can only be picked up by conscious entity and by aware beings. Wherever consciousness exists in the universe, when the vibration appears, it will be picked up. It takes mind to become aware of vibrations and the mind is a function of induction from the foundation of solar systems. The Universe is inductive, for the whole universe is in open communication and, at the same time, consciously aware, not just on earth but all throughout the universe. The greatest inductive source we know is the sun whose rays are felt from extremely far. We are aware of the potential of our solar system, and to live near its inductive nature, you need protection.

Anything that is inductive is destructive by nature. Existence ensures that life is protected from inductive sources, including life on this planet via cosmic organization. It is common knowledge that the planets protect earth, not only from asteroids, but their collective positioning are such that they balance the entire solar system. Earth orbits the sun at the precise distance that allows life to flourish on this planet as well as life could not be possible without the canopy that nourishes all the life forms above and below. However, man has developed technologies able to destroy not only themselves but the entire planet. Since the sun is able to destroy human life, we are provided protection from its energies, or else it becomes a destructive center for all life on earth, even though itself is the source for the propagation of life. Who can protect humanity from itself other than for humanity to awaken from its slumber, from its sleep and lack of consciousness awareness.

Humanity cannot live in a harmonized fashion while at the same time decoding information from two inductive centers without being confused or destroyed. There must always be a protective barrier between inductive centers. Imagine the earth centered between two solar systems of equidistance. In such a state, planet rotation would be of no value, for it would be eternally daytime, and as such, this mode of existence would simply be a time triangle. Our modern technologies have inundated all cultures and we are centered between not only technologies of old, but also new and evolving technologies.

In this modern technological era, engineers and programmers who work with artificial intelligence are working hard to develop capabilities to remove spiritual barriers connecting you to your spirit life and spiritual essence, which serve as the canopy that protects you from the slew of technologies inundating society. Once these A.I. systems are capable of fluidizing, controlling, and limiting your spiritual essence, humanity will fall apart. Modern technological systems are controlled fields that do not align to your essence nor the nature of consciousness—they are absolutes, and nothing is absolute. Impact from external inductive centers able to control you destroy the mind, and to destroy the mind is not only to destroy matter, but the mind is the seat, the bridge between your physical presence and the Real— what most call God. To destroy the mind is to create a vacuum, followed by the inevitable collapse.

We live in a world bombarded by fields from many different sources, not only solar fields but radio stations, television stations, cell phone towers, etc., but you have to understand that fields are deterministic as defined by their sources, thus can be blind in many areas as a result of their ability to keep you linear. Understand what is meant by the ability to keep you linear. Most of the youth do not know how life functioned prior to the mass commercialization of cell phones and the globalization of the internet. These two systems have digitalized how we function—a direct result of some of the chaos and consequences we see today.

The moment you become linear in thinking, it becomes difficult to find the way out once you are caught in the currents of the fields and as such you live with constraints. Living with constraints makes life seem deterministic, which robs you of your free will as constraints tend to maximize the need for a stimulus-response existence. The mind, the sun, and your consciousness are crucial foundations that must be understood for you cannot wield any of them and yet are very powerful. Understand, that which you are not able to wield is the base of your stability, therefore, is that which you need to tune into, is that which you need to understand, for their true essence does not accumulate yet weighs heavy, they are the foundation for life on earth, and when you understand them, they will always shine for you. Unknown energy fields can be perceived during meditation via conscious awareness.

Consciousness is that which belongs to the cosmic whole, and via meditation, you learn to calibrate the ebbs and flows of your inductive mind to its stillness and beauty. The nature of that which is inductive, whether in you or external to you, will always be wrong if you try to map it, for its energy is eternally morphing. If you try mapping the endpoint of ocean waves at the beach by placing a marker, you will be proven wrong every second, every minute, every hour, every day, every year, then you realize you are not only destroying but also wasting your energy.

Through identification with material existence, the merry-go-round spins faster, you move faster away from reality, the energy goes on crashing, yet your consciousness remains dormant. You move further away from love for you can no longer be aware of dangers, thereby inviting the worst form of duality. Psychological boundary dissolution kills identification with the material order, it births awareness in the individual, the point from where consciousness expansion can begin. This is what the Upanishads meant by being "established in the sun of awareness, the only true lamp."

Consciousness seeks no identity and thus is never destroyed. It remains a blank screen, a mutual assurance that propagates life and ensures the quality of the whole. In our modern culture, society identifies with control, that which is constantly at war, doing so, all the rust and true concerns of the whole remain invisible until the collapse. Control has a limited time before becoming obsolescence and thus has a limited scope, but human psychology cannot see the obsession with control that brings about wars and torture to the human spirit. Every decade has its own flavor, each decade is a sort of cultural shift, yet it goes unseen by most, and while entrenched in the culture of said decades, we go on creating unnecessary problems.

Differentiation is an opening, a guiding light, provided it is in tune with the way. Man has perverted almost all differences. Differentiation leading to clarity is the true guiding light, just as consciousness, which embodies all, contains the true image, the true understanding of the collectivity of existence. To ask when did the soul enter the body is akin to asking while building a house, when did space enter the area around that you found the walls. It was always there. The problem with humanity is that we only see form, we see only thoughts, and to look at light, in time you want to destroy it for its intensity outweighs you, it is blinding, it is heavy, it overpowers your consciousness.

True illumination is the spark of consciousness that distances you away from duality—the realization that you cannot imitate the light. Realizing that, you simply let go allowing life to renew, allowing consciousness to be and unfold in the here and now in its dissolute formlessness. An ultimate dissolution implies the inability to put yourself back together in the old sense of how you were. You become a nothingness, and in this nothingness, true composition lies beyond your abilities, and you have fallen. This fall is not in the physical sense but a unification with or an approach towards the real, it is more like a rise.

Sri Ramana Maharshi tells us, "Complete surrender to God means giving up all thoughts and to concentrate on Him. If we can concentrate on him, all other thoughts disappear. If the actions of the mind, speech, and body are merged with God, all the burdens of our life will be on him." This is truly a cosmic shift, and in that state, you are not present in the physical sense. The oceanic feel is then the bridge between the physical reality of space-time and the cosmic ocean. You have to put

161

yourself in your own revolution to cancel all other revolutions that seek to destroy you and trap you. This is a type of parallelism that allows you to develop internal qualities to not be pulled away, thereby discarding any memory that will throw you off and seek to pull you under. You have to be careful though, for parallelism will destroy you unless you're able to move parallel while uncovering your own internal substance able to capture your own imagination, to unfold that which is hidden in you. This prevents you from acting or responding to stimuli but moves you beyond the mind via observation of the mind and your thoughts. Stimuli without interaction is an impingement on your physiological system, for there can be no stimuli without interaction. This is well known in physics as there can be no friction without rubbing, meaning without the flowing of electrons, for it is electron flow which applies pressure. Having developed internal qualities, you have created a type of flow state, a type of psychological fluidization that you can use to create. Anything you fluidize, you stand on. The opposite is true as well for if you allow others to fluidize your mind, they stand on you. Hence the weight and burden of feeling low sometimes. Putting yourself in a revolution, your flow state becomes primary and all others secondary, thus they cannot induce a pull on you, allowing you to maintain your integrity. This prevents unwanted memory, which can induce a response to form in you that destroys your individuality.

To maintain your individuality, learn to self-actualize an internal revolution that moves you away from negative energy, or else you become dependent forever, you become a robot. Know that everything you move away from can be pinpointed, and bring it into focus. In it, or it in you, you can sense it. However, to localize it, you have to move away from it.

You have to see it in its orbit and you in yours, then balance is maintained. Life at the local level starts out with infinite divisibility for that is the only way the localized consciousness can develop language, by moving things around. This is the way it can see itself, temporal dimensional interplay. "In every dimension, there is infinite space to run," and you have to recognize, you have to see that your intelligence is multidimensional. That's how the brain generates thought and creates languages, by seeing motion. Physical motion releases certain abilities in the brain that allow you to create meaning.

When external forces, which are greater than you, can induce a response from you, you will be formatted, you will lose the quality of your mind and your thoughts will no longer be yours, for they will be induced from fields external to you. In moments of creativity where the mind is still, essence from decoded fields is present in you. You are not aware of them for you have not developed the ability to pull from them because they are subtle. Your uniqueness rises from your ability to uncover your subtle nature and guide it. Uniqueness, if fully developed, will recognize essences. You will craft, you will create, and you will become the artist. When uniqueness is developed, the ego is minimized and brought to its proper function, but most artistically talented people are too individualistic and lose their uniqueness.

Do not confuse uniqueness for individualism. Individuality, though a pillar and crucial for you to understand who you are, is juvenile by nature. It binds and thus blocks out major components of reality. You have to move away from individuality and into uniqueness. Uniqueness has meditative qualities, uniqueness is graceful in nature, and uniqueness is in tune with the way. Essence in you, derived from your uniqueness is that which you fluidize. I cannot see it for you, nor can anyone else see it for you, but one thing is certain, your fluidized essence will serve the whole, it will serve the common good. The beauty of the mind is that it can present all qualities hidden and non-hidden. But if there are sensations in the body, those sensations kill the qualities first, then kills the mind, then the consciousness goes, turning you into a reactive animal as the stimulus response has now taken over your motor function in the body. The stimulus response is a function of externality and that which lives on boundaries.

Memory is geographical, the Bible is geographical, the Koran is geographical. You cannot assign geography to spirituality for spirituality is of consciousness awareness, out of which springs your quality, your creativity, and your uniqueness. Geography is a known, which can be reduced to a point. All is unknown until developed and moves backwards in time. Memory is a dead thing. Imagine modern day society running Microsoft DOS in modern times. Yet this is religion, stuck in the geography of discomfort in contrast to the nature of truth and reality, which is a constant sea of change. Geography is simply control. In such a mind state, you need stimulants. Expanding to the light weighs you down, you become matter, hence the eternal quest for liberation. It must be realized individually—no gods can give you liberation for it is birth of freedom. It is quality that is undeniable, it is the quality in each thing that leads to the collective non-differentiable that is undeniable. This quality exists in every light being, it exists wherever light exists, it exists wherever light penetrates. It must guide the light. Yes, the light is visible and the consciousness is not. Internally, the consciousness field can either be a single tree or it can be a forest. Sometimes I go for long walks on wooded trails and I cannot help being fascinated by the beauty of nature and her secrets, revealed only to her true lovers and elevated above those who are blind. It is arduous work to understand the mind and its infinite flow states, but nature provides us with some clues. Looking at trees in winter, the bare branches and their numerous bifurcations resemble rivers flowing and reaching for the sky. Likewise, the mind contains an infinite number of flow states that link us to all in existence, yet these flow states remain dormant and mostly unknown to many of you.

When you can understand that the mind is like a tree that turns into a forest with infinite flow states, you will seek understanding and you will flourish. By flourishing, you will grow and expand. This expansion is not of the exhaustive nature of work but one of solace where you are settled in your being, in deep connection with your spirit's life. All of you have sat under a tree during summer and have walked on wooded trails that shield you from the intensity of the sun. These feelings are also manifested internally from consciousness expansion, ones where no explanation is possible and difficult to put to words. Feelings that embody life in ways that bring existence to your doorsteps. In time, via deep meditative practices, the mind expands and becomes an ocean and a forest. When your conscious awareness expands to that of cosmic understanding as an ocean or a forest, the ego is no longer a barrier and is brought to its proper function in an almost non-existent state.

The expansiveness of the quality of mind determines the number of vibrations and quality emanating from its field. Seek to develop understanding, to develop a mind that turns your light inwards to prevent external conflicts that can destroy you. Whenever a greater light overpowers your light, it will bind you with shame and guilt. You need to gain your knowledge and understanding from mother nature. Mind cannot live with shame and guilt looped ad infinitum for they become anchors and you must drop them both to free yourself. If you do not drop them both, it is your consciousness that dies. It is your consciousness you lose and it is your quality that has been taken away from you.

All lights are already canceled; therefore, consciousness does not bother. They are cancelled because they are supposed to balance each other and not be in conflict. If you disregard your consciousness or let your consciousness die, it never returns to the body. It is only when you trap the infinite void, the infinite darkness in a revolution that light is manifested and presents itself. If you take a Tibetan singing bowl and bang it, sound presents itself, for the medium exist that allows it to be. I remember when my son was born, the doctor tapped him in the butt and right away he awakened with a cry. That tap resonated through a medium, his body, and the memory induced a cry, awakening the consciousness in the local plane.

We are the void, consciousness in human form, the light, observing the universe. Light is never manifested without those waiting to sense it on a particular path. The sole function of light is to illuminate pathways. On earth, when you are alive, the void, the consciousness is in form of light, and when you die, your consciousness is freed and returns to source. Light is simply an intensity, a portal, and you sometimes hear of people talking about seeing bright light in near-death experiences. I presume this is because they have not lived a life that allows them to be freed from this physical plane. The consciousness available in the local energy field is in a small ratio compared to all light sources. Though the energy to consciousness ratio is of greater significant value, it can never exhaust the consciousness in it. Beyond the locality, consciousness encompasses all space and time. Out of it emerges space and time.

There is no path to enlightenment that brings you to the door of the divine, that is like asking for the path of the forest to take to full bloom. To arrive at your own forest, you have to expand while maintaining your non-differentiable quality, this quality is a knowing—like all forests being green and all oceans being salty. Only you know your own path to such quality and only consciousness can lead you to the ocean. No one outside of you can guide you, for when consciousness dies, the energy has no use and is consumed. When you understand that every word and every step one takes is a form of division, you become less active and not more, you become silent and simply observe.

You have to see that, by nature, you are your own division. You, by nature, are your own source of power and your own source of destruction, therefore, you also possess the capacity to be your own source for unifying not only your energy but also to move closer to consciousness. Learn how to drop thought and form, that which brings guilt and shame, to move to clarity so that you can unite your consciousness from the local realm to that of the comic realm, bringing your psychology to wholeness. This is meditation, a form of centering, as it is observed in nature. Meditation moves you away from mind, away from differences, and into spaciousness. Temporal differentiation is an opening into clarity, that differentiation becomes a mechanical function when unconsciously unaware. That which is mechanical is the most painful form of division, a robot, a thing, no attractive quality, hence the dangers of thought to split you.

To be mechanical is to be a zombie, and when a system is mechanical, no part can question whether the integrity of the system supports the collective. This is dangerous, this is not life, and the mechanization of life destroys all quality. You can tell from experience that existence will never divide and fracture without first considering wholeness. You have to learn to become one with existence even in the face of your greatest fear. This is the giving birth principle—existence never fractures from the external and has a positive consequence because wholeness is an internal function. The greatest trick existence plays on you is the fact that you are different, that difference at a surface level is a psychological hindrance, bringing out all sorts of insecurities and problems for yourself. It is these insecurities that have led to everything being weaponized, magnifying fear in society, and leading everyone to search for salvation irrespective of the impact on the collective. In the quantization of life, nothing can have dignity, hence the dangers of science and its ability to falsify how your reality is perceived.

To quantify is destructive. When you are unable to quantify, you become destructive. Where then does the problem lie? It's you. You are afraid to simply be. The inability to quantify is you being open to existence, it is you letting go of fear, it is you taking responsibility, it is you accepting the challenges of life, it is you accepting grace by remaining whole. This is your opportunity. All exists here and now, and they simply present themselves when the time is right—some with the same fear, some with the same insecurities. No one creates anything other than that creation is found within, you only need to open yourself to intelligence. The problem is that being a conscious being, you are not a thing, you are not an object, for only objects and things are quantized. This is your challenge, reconciling that constant split between the energy that pulls or pushes on you and aligning it to consciousness awareness. It is obvious that infinite division is a unitary collapse in place, a sort of distortion able to bring anything to a halt and the opposite of which if you can conserve information, allows you to bring existence down to earth. It allows existence to center on you as you transcend duality. But most likely, it will destroy you, for infinite division is infinite differentiation and infinite differentiation is infinite scale, of which your mind can no longer function accordingly.

Irrespective of how that comes about, to move away from this collapse and distortion, to remain whole, you need to bring your psychology to a state of non-differentiability. Infinite differences in the physical form, you can easily scoop it away, but if psychological, this division is a completely different matter as it will require a unification of all your intelligence to arrive. If integrity is your utmost value, you will find a way to move beyond any illusion, whether real or false, and not compromise yourself during momentary illusions. To compromise your integrity and to accept forces that are contrary to your natural state of existence is to compromise your ground of being, to destroy your consciousness.

Chapter 9

The Stillness of Reality

Consciousness is your ground of being and your ground of being is your compass to your true center. When you are truly centered, you expand your consciousness awareness to liberate your psychology and free you of negative karma. Last week, as I was riding my bike and going to the gym, I noticed in the horizon how all the trees were green, everything was lined up perfectly, and it was as if it was difficult to differentiate the different types of trees—which were oak trees and which were spruce trees. Being summertime in Florida, this time of year, everything looks green and really nice. It dawned on me to ask—how can you track something

175

without the ability to differentiate? The inability to track something brings the mind to stillness, no motion, a sort of blank you can call truth, stability, but that can become confusing if you are pre-conditioned to always extract something or to differentiate, for to differentiate is to track and see delineation.

To track something implies the understanding of a relationship, a sort of resonance, a male and female dancing in search of synchronization, for like charges cannot resonate, thus are non-differentiable, therefore, cannot dance the language of existence. The beauty of dance, of resonance are revealed when the two steps fall in tune and replicate themselves. What makes love a dance is its ability to replicate itself, to excite consciousness, to invite life, and to have the sense of complete clarity, the boundless feeling, the sense of falling. Love in physical existence is to preserve uniqueness, to bring two opposites into one and there cannot be uniqueness without this form of love. Conservation of uniqueness is the purest quality of love, all that is unique vibrates in such a way that weaves nouveau patterns discernable only by future generations.

Uniqueness vibrates the life energy, which lies beyond the bound nature of the mind.

You have to not confuse what it is to be living with life and living with the collective unity. Yes, we are living. Yes, we are alive. But life, and to understand life, is a completely different phenomenon. The ability to differentiate is possible only when differences in wave forms present themselves, and beyond that, we are completely clueless. For life and its sources are beyond form. Differentiating the non-differentiable at the local level exposes all form of uniqueness. We know that no one ever likes uniqueness, for it is a unification of two opposites, leaving behind both of the old, that which is known as well as that which has become knowledge, it has made them obsolete as it moves closer and closer to non-differentialness, true stability, true wholeness able to bring them into a flow state in tune with the way. Existence is always a mystery, and love is the energy that keeps it so. Non-differentiable is immovable, all powerful. Non-differentiability promotes an infinite possibility of uniqueness. Non-differentiability is not that you look at two things where you clearly see the difference and pretend that you do not see color. Non-differentiability is to arrive at the center, to be at the center of that which is, the projection center, consciousness.

Nature goes to great lengths to conceal its differentiability, for too much perceive differentiation collapses the system. Look at the night sky, look at the sky during the day, all in unison. Look at the stars, look at the ocean, all in unison, true non-differentialness, wholeness you can say. To create differentiable sources is to spark destructive energies that collapse systems. Non-differentiability dissolves patterns at the conscious level. This is why I ask, how do you track something without the ability to differentiate? To differentiate does not mean to identify differences between physical objects, but to differentiate is to see depth, to see flow, to see boundlessness. We understand that no crystallization and no expansion happens for no reason. We also see how going from a pond to a lake, and a lake to an ocean helps in understanding communication from forces that lie far beyond. Beyond all those forms of communication lies the atmosphere, a greater sense of feeling of vastness that contains its own mode of communication. Understand that there is always greater clarity, clarity that the mind cannot comprehend for it is beyond form.

Clarity is a result of a flow regime in tune with the intelligence of life, therefore, when viewed and analyzed, you get the sense of a perpetual fall. To imagine the sense of a perpetual fall, take the mind and bring it into a void. When clarity exists beyond the comprehension of the mind, the void and the speed at which it operates humbles our knowledge. Thus, knowledge remains incomplete as we can never be one hundred percent in sync with the over-arching intelligence that lies beyond us. The source of the ultimate intelligence is unknown and unknowable; therefore, many cultures have a different name for this source. Thereby giving you total responsibility for your life. Through spirituality and meditative practices, you develop the sense of knowing, the knowing from the silence that brings in harmony that helps you in any situation and difficulty. Non-differentiability is to arrive at wholeness. This is the foundation of true spirituality, a uniqueness birthed from within that only you can understand.

Always focus the mind on that which leads you to a non-differentiable state of being, making you whole and not divided among yourself. To live in clarity is to perpetually be falling, and consciousness always lives in clarity and thus in this phenomenal plane, it is always moving away from form to form, never knowing what comes next. Understand that you are a conscious being and you too also live in clarity. To live in clarity is an immense responsibility, to live in clarity is to accept your vulnerability in the vastness of existence. You cannot be fearful of perceived thoughts that seek to divide your psyche, for the responsibility is yours to gain knowledge of your brain, and you must work on it sooner than later, you must live in truth and not fear, and by living in truth, you will come to know how to weave the quality that gives your life a flavor unique to you. Osho tells us that tomorrow is the day that never comes, and if you read the Treasured Writings of Khalil Gibran, you will know that tomorrow never leaves its secrets in the book of eternity. How can you not see that any hope of tomorrow is to forget your responsibility today, here and now? When tomorrow comes, it can only be here and now.

To live here and now today is to author your story in the book of life, to face the mystery of existence with the courage to know that your presence is a necessary condition upon which tomorrow hinges. Your developed quality today is the fragrance that gives tomorrow its confidence. Your developed quality is the flaming of a candle, burning away memory. Memory can be painful, for memory is form, for memory is the experience of forms interacting, and when form becomes a symbol that troubles your psychology, it is the expansion of consciousness that clears the way, and you have to be willing to let go completely to unite your psyche. Memory is remembrance and remembrance is a function of coordinates, consciousness has no coordinates, thus there can never be remembrance, only uniqueness once the awareness is present in form.

You cannot apply coordinates to the boundless, you cannot fix its position nor divide it. Where does remembrance come from? By letting go of memory, you move beyond the mind and into wholeness, you are closer to the here and now than to dragging the memories of the past. Memory is partial, memory is a control, hence why it is painful and allowing any form of partiality to weigh on you, you quickly reach a local-minima, a focused hell, an unimpeded impingement on the body-mind. Letting go is when grace enters, the precondition of which is complete and total kindness towards all life forms, even in the face of your worst obstacle or fear. To know that memory is form is to know that some memories weigh heavily on you if you do not know how to burn the candle of life and if you do not know how to live in the Tao. Becoming consciously aware helps you drop all psychological forms that weigh on the mind. It helps you drop all thought, and helps you move in silence and in truth.

Truth is born from silence—the depth of the conscious field of existence that observes life through you. No two individuals can have the same truth, for the depths that they draw from are different. Burn through your memories with the candle of life, the here and now, so the truth can prevail, so you can free yourself. The future you are seeking is found by releasing the fragrance from your burning candle. Having kindled your candle, having kindled your memories, you will have learned that nothing goes anywhere, therefore, you are the light that lights a thousand candles. You will learn that your nothingness is the unification of duality, bringing two poles together, and when the two poles are indivisibly one, you become the light of consciousness. You are now the Buddha, the Jesus, and the OSHO. Do not be afraid of letting the light of your consciousness shine, for it is through shining that the weight and heaviness of the material existence are lifted off your shoulders. Understand, without the presence of form, the concept of creation cannot be materialized.

The concept of creation is the root of all negative differentiation—a blocker to understanding the nature of consciousness. To talk creation, each difference would have to be of a different source from the cosmic whole, thus cannot be of "God" as proclaimed in the Bible. Creation being that which is known to you in the physical realm is only a minute portion of the whole potential—

you can say a true differential whose endpoints are not conceivable by the mind. For that would allow it greater access. Osho reminds us that for Creation to be true, the theory of evolution must be false and vice versa. How can evolution be true when a "perfect God" created the world? He reminds us that evolution is a continual improvement on that which God has created. Thus, either creation is false or evolution is false, but through meditation and the knowledge of self, you come to realize they are both false. Both the Bible and Darwin are false. Without consciousness awareness, anything done with the mind has an element of hate, which can override all quality.

The suns and stars are the eyes of the Ultimate nondual, and all life which is fractal in nature follows the function of the eye, the sun, in the localized field. The suns and stars being the eyes of God peering into the eternal darkness is a stark reminder of being too attached to duality, to materialism, to science without borders and the consequences thereof. The light will always cast a shadow and that shadow reminds you of two things—one is to remind you of the source of your function, and the second is to remind you of the function from the source the light itself comes from. You are that which you are a function of. If a shadow brings you fear, then it is wrong at the source it comes from. We all cast shadows and the question becomes, how can you be afraid of yourself?

The forest and the ocean serve as reminders of natural flow states that are focal points in tune with the way life flourishes in them. These two focal points balance each other. You have to see that it is you that is centering, the moon and the sun. Though they themselves are focal points, they are in tune with the way. They do not destroy, they simply awaken. All that you bring to focus will destroy you if not in tune with the way, and be a source of abundance when in tune with the way. I cannot think that animals like cats and dogs can bring the sun and the moon to a focus in a destructive fashion. Only humans are capable of that. Awaken to consciousness awareness.

Made in United States
North Haven, CT
25 September 2023

41969750R00102